George Yancey

BEYOND
RACIAL
GRIDLOCK

Embracing Mutual Responsibility

IVP Books

An imprint of InterVarsity Press
Downers Grove, Illinois

InterVarsity Press
P.O. Box 1400, Downers Grove, IL 60515-1426
World Wide Web: www.ivpress.com
E-mail: mail@ivpress.com

InterVarsity Press® is the book-publishing division of InterVarsity Christian Fellowship/USA®, a student movement active on campus at hundreds of universities, colleges and schools of nursing in the United States of America, and a member movement of the International Fellowship of Evangelical Students. For information about local and regional activities, write Public Relations Dept., InterVarsity Christian Fellowship/USA, 6400 Schroeder Rd., P.O. Box 7895, Madison, WI 53707-7895, or visit the IVCF website at <www.intervarsity.org>.

All Scripture quotations, unless otherwise indicated, are taken from the Holy Bible, New International Version®. NIV®. Copyright ©1973, 1978, 1984 by International Bible Society. Used by permission of Zondervan Publishing House. All rights reserved.

Design: Cindy Kiple

Images: Martin Barraud/Getty Images

ISBN-10: 0-8308-3376-5
ISBN-13: 978-0-8308-3376-4

Printed in the United States of America ∞

Library of Congress Cataloging-in-Publication Data

Yancey, George A., 1962-
  Beyond racial gridlock: embracing mutual responsibility / George
Yancey.
      p. cm.
  Includes bibliographical references.
  ISBN-13: 978-0-8308-3376-4 (pbk.: alk. paper)
  ISBN-10: 0-8308-3376-5 (pbk.: alk. paper)
  1. Race relations—Religious aspects—Christianity. 2.
Reconciliation—Religious aspects—Christianity. 3. United
States—Race relations. I. Title.
BT734.2.Y37 2006
270.089—dc22

                                                              2005033142

P   19   18   17   16   15

Y   21   20

Contents

Introduction

With every passing year, a few more gray hairs appear in my mane. These hairs are both welcomed and feared. They are feared because they remind me of my declining physical abilities. But they are welcomed because they help me to look my age. I have been both blessed and cursed with a youthful appearance. After college I spent a year substitute teaching. The regular teachers often mistook me for a high school student, and once for a junior high student.

Perhaps my appearance explains why, until recently, I often heard a sound familiar to black men under the age of thirty: KA-CHUNK! It is the sound of car doors locking. I have heard this sound as I walked through a parking lot and even as a car whizzed past me at forty mph. It is a sound of the fear which whites still feel toward blacks in our society. It is a sound which represents the higher incarceration rates of blacks and the beating of Rodney King. It is a sound which many black men come to hate. And make no mistake about it: it is a sound reserved for black men. When I asked my sociology students about the sound of car doors locking, black men were the only ones who had heard it, with one exception, a Puerto Rican female.

I point out the phenomenon of locked car doors to suggest that we have not come as far as we like to think in our attempts to eradicate our racist past. Have our society's problems of racism gone away? Clearly not. Are we still trapped by racial prejudice and discrimination, more than forty years after the enactment of the great civil rights legislation? Yes, as the locking of car doors demonstrates. Can the next generation of Americans improve on the previous generation's record of racial healing? Perhaps, but there is no guarantee of improvement. I often ask my students for answers to the racial problems we have discussed in class. They sometimes argue that when younger folks grow up, they will not have the prejudice of older Americans. I respect their conviction. But I suspect that college students in the 1960s probably felt the same way.

If we are going to solve the problem of race in our society, I am convinced that we must make an intentional effort. We did make a strong intentional effort in the 1960s through the development of civil rights legislation. Perhaps laws and regulations have brought us as far as they can. Laws and regulations, while good and necessary, are not enough. Unless we can get at the soul of our nation, we will remain mired in the garbage of racism.

As Christians, if we are to touch the soul of this nation, we must look to our faith. We must recognize the spiritual problems that racism creates for us. Christians have a responsibility to play a significant role in bringing about a future free from the pain of racism. Our Christian history is a mixture of triumph and failure in this area. For example, Christians supported the movement for the abolition of slavery, but they also pressured Native Americans to give up their own culture. We cannot alter our past successes or failures. We can only look to the shaping of our future race relations.

What does our Christian faith offer to help solve these problems? Is there a unique Christian solution, different from any of our society's secular alternatives? Or must Christians try to solve the problems of racism in precisely the same way as non-Christians? If that is the case, then can Christians profess to have anything unique to offer to help solve one of the most important moral issues of our day?

The problem of racism is the problem of sin. It requires not only a political remedy but a spiritual remedy as well. Racial issues are about how we treat each other, and our relationships with each other are clearly of concern to God. If this is true, then Christians have much to say about how we treat people of different races. We have moral and spiritual insight which can help our fellow Americans deal with racial issues. Unfortunately, all too often we have relied on secular solutions instead of searching our own faith for answers. To find answers that are distinctively Christian, we must be honest about our own biases. We must take an honest look at the Scriptures.

A PARALLEL: THE MORAL ISSUE OF ABORTION

Racism is not the only moral issue that confronts Christians in our society. The most publicized issue is abortion. Research indicates that a person's position on abortion is related to the person's religious faith.[1] Those without a strong faith are likely to dismiss the moral questions that surround abortion. For them abortion is a procedure undergone by women who feel that they are not ready for motherhood. Perhaps the question of fetal viability raises the question of the extent of a mother's rights in the later stages of the pregnancy, but most people with a low priority on religious faith support abortion within the first three months of pregnancy.

Christians, however, generally hold a contrasting perspective on abortion. Most Christians do not regard life as something that begins at a point of fetal viability. God gives all life. In the eyes of believers, the age of the fetus does not make it more human or less human. God, rather than the ability to live without biological assistance, gives human beings value; therefore Christians must challenge the affront of abortion. While Christians debate possible justifications for abortion (rape, incest, to protect the life of the mother) they hold a general consensus about the evil of this practice. For this reason, even Christians such as black evangelicals who are politically liberal on other issues still tend to oppose abortion.

Of course we cannot say that all Christians oppose abortion, any more than we can say that all non-Christians support it. Christians may find reasons to support abortion despite the concept of God-given human worth, and non-Christians may find secular arguments to oppose the practice.[2] But research has shown that Christian belief is a major force behind resistance to abortion in the United States.[3] Clearly our Christian theology has helped us formulate a perspective on abortion which differs from the perspective of those who lack a strong Christian worldview. How Christians have responded to abortion demonstrates that Christianity may provide a distinctive stance toward a moral issue.

What does this mean for the larger society? Evangelical and Catholic Christians have been at the forefront of the prolife movement and are promoting a distinctively Christian solution to the thorny issue of abortion. But when we look at most European countries, we find no strong Christian-based prolife movement; in fact, there is an almost total absence of resistance to abortion. The contrast is to be expected when we consider that residents of Europe tend to have a lower level of Christian faith than residents of the United States.[4] Clearly the argument over abortion in the United States has taken a different shape because believers decided to develop a distinctively Christian perspective on the issue.

The Moral Issue of Race

It is perfectly appropriate that a Christian perspective does exist for a moral issue such as abortion. Often, however, we are too restrictive about what constitutes a moral issue. In graduate school I attended a Bible study which focused on Christian answers for the important moral issues of the day. The leader emphasized that we must be willing to engage the culture on moral issues such as abortion, homosexuality and euthanasia. Racism was not addressed at all.[5] When I expressed my concerns to the college pastor, it was clear that he did not think of racism as a moral issue. It was not a coincidence that a predominately white church sponsored the Bible study.

Racial issues are moral issues. Even if a distinctively Christian solution is not acceptable to the larger secular culture, we must engage that culture with ideas based on our faith. We may not be able to win the day with our engagement, but our activity will help us to alter the debate, just as our involvement has altered the debate over abortion.

In order to engage our society with a Christian perspective on racism, we have to determine what that perspective is. We must examine the theological tenets of our faith and allow our faith to form our ideas.[6] If our faith is built on values beyond this world, then we should be able to draw on those values to construct a solution unique among all the other solutions offered by the larger society. With the help of Christian scholars and theologians, ordinary Christian believers will begin to understand how their faith should influence their approach to racial issues.[7] If the moral issue of abortion serves as a valid example, then we can offer solutions which demonstrate to the larger secular society that Christians hold a radically different perspective on racial issues.

IMITATION OF SECULAR MODELS

My reading of secular and Christian literature on issues of race has not uncovered any unique stance on the part of the Christian church. When Christians write and speak about racial issues, they sound much like their secular counterparts. Instead of initiating our own solutions to the problem of racism, we merely copy the solutions offered by the rest of the world. We use the Bible to support our own biases and presuppositions rather than looking to the Bible to transcend our moral limitations. Christians argue with other Christians about racial issues as much as non-Christians argue with each other because the solutions we propose are based not on intrinsic Christian values but on more worldly presuppositions.

Because of the way we mimic the rest of society, Christianity does not appear to offer any unique solution to racism. It appears that the best Christians can do is to pick and choose from the ideas of the larger society. Christians can get on board with the best of these solutions, but we will never be leaders in the search for solutions.

I am not a painter. But I imagine that for a painter to do the best job possible, he or she must have paints for all possible colors. I suppose a great painter can still do a good job even if some colors are missing, but the finished work will not be as expressive as it would have been if all colors of paint had been available. The picture will be incomplete.

Secular answers to racism are not so much wrong as incomplete. The proposed solutions may do some good, but there are missing elements, or colors, in the pictures they paint. Those missing colors reflect the lack of a spiritual focus. By adding our Christian voices to the discussion, we can bring forth the colors necessary for a complete painting. We can add the missing elements to the attempts to overcome racism.

A UNIQUE SOLUTION

Christians must begin to take the leadership role because our faith offers a unique answer to racism. If we can take the moral lead, we will provide a powerful witness to all those who are frustrated by racial problems in the United States. There could be few greater miracles in our society than to find a solution for racial alienation. Even the most skeptical doubters may reconsider their religious cynicism if we offer real answers to racial strife.[8]

I contend that there is a unique Christian perspective different from the solutions offered by the non-Christian world. Do I have that solution? I am only one Christian in academia. I dare not speak for the entire body of Christ. We need dialogue among many Christians to begin to develop a faith-based voice. I intend to make a strong argument that our Christian values provide us with unique solutions to the problem of racism.

To understand how best to eliminate racism, I propose that we start with the Christian doctrine of human depravity. Secular solutions to racism are incomplete because they ignore the reality of human depravity and our sin nature. In this book I will develop what I term a mutual responsibility model of racial healing, which recognizes how the poison of human depravity affects all people.

Christians may agree or disagree with my arguments about racism. In the same way, some believers may disagree with the traditional Christian perspective on abortion. But the traditional Christian perspective has emerged through decades of debate, and it represents what a high percentage of Christians think about abortion. Nonbelievers at least know where most Christians stand on this issue. If my arguments about how Christian faith applies to racism are incorrect, then we must engage in an active debate about better solutions. But the debate must be in the context of our Christian faith so we develop a coherent set of ideas. Then the world will see an answer which they can accept or reject.

IMPLICATIONS OF OFFERING A CHRISTIAN SOLUTION

During a teleconference with a book club that was reading my first book,[9] I was asked a thoughtful question about what Christians can do about racial issues. The questioner pointed out that even if Christians find solutions to racism, non-Christians may not feel obligated to follow those solutions. And while most people in our society may call themselves Christians, we know that only a fraction take their faith seriously enough to change their actions. So even if we find biblical answers to the racial issues in our society, will it make a difference?

My answer to that question is yes. To understand why I believe that our solutions will matter, we must look at our own history. For example, the abolitionist movement in the United States developed, for the most part, out of the early Quaker churches[10] and was buttressed by other Christians until the end of slavery was achieved.[11] The women's suffrage movement was greatly aided by the works of many Christian women church leaders.[12]

Of course there were Christians who opposed abolition and women's suffrage. However, Christian activists were key players in the great reform movements. These movements created a lasting impact on society because a critical mass of Christians used their Christian faith to reevaluate slavery and the voting rights of women.[13] If we can develop a similar critical mass about race, we will also have a lasting impact on society.

After we conceptualize a Christian answer to racial problems, we have a responsibility to articulate our ideas to the larger society. We may fear that others will not want to hear what we have to say. But I believe that our society will be more open to our solutions than we might expect. Who is not tired of racial hostility? Who would not want to listen to new and innovative ideas about how to end the hostility? The task is important, not because we want to weigh in with politically correct notions about racism, but in order to do the foundational work of racial healing. Bringing estranged people together is a fitting work for those of us who claim to follow Christ.

MY APPROACH IN THIS BOOK

In the first five chapters of this book I will explore secular solutions to the problem of racism. We have to understand what others have tried and why their answers are incomplete before we can formulate new answers. In the last six chapters I will try to construct what I believe is a Christian model, the mutual responsibility model, for dealing with racism.

In chapter one I will explore the two contrasting views about racism prevalent among Americans. In the first view, racism is something overt which is done by one individual to another. In the second view, racism is structural as well as individualistic; social institutions can perpetuate racism even when individuals do not intend to be racist.

I will end chapter one with a brief introduction to the four general models of how people have tried to solve racism in the United States. In chapters two through five I will examine each of the four models—colorblindness, Anglo-conformity, multiculturalism and white responsibility—in greater depth.

In chapter six I will begin my construction of a Christian solution. I believe that a true Christian solution must take our sin nature into account. To this end I will introduce the mutual responsibility model and will elaborate on it throughout the rest of the book. In chapters seven and eight I will look at how our sin nature contributes to the way European Americans and racial minorities perpetuate racial alienation in the United States. In chapter nine I will show how Jesus, the ultimate reconciler, dealt with those who were ethnically different from himself. In chapter ten I will discuss how human depravity contributes to racial fears in our society. Finally, in chapter eleven I will discuss the implications of a Christian mutual responsibility model and end this book by examining some ways Christians can rethink their practices and institutions in light of my proposed Christian-based answer to racism in the United States.

PART ONE

Four Secular Models
of Dealing with Racism

1

Two Views of Racism

When we tackle the subject of racism, a huge issue that confronts us is our inability to talk with each other. I am not referring to immigrants who speak Spanish, Mandarin, Portuguese or some other language. I mean that even those of us who understand English often use the same words or phrases to mean different things when we talk about race. For Christians to be a part of the racial healing process, we have to deal with these contrasting definitions and the confusion they cause.

Perhaps the most important distinction between people of different races is the way we understand the concept of racism. Christians should not be surprised by the tendency to define racial problems differently. Such a self-serving tendency comes from our human desire to escape our own responsibility and/or to gain resources from others in society.

THE IMPORTANCE OF DEFINING RACISM

The way we define a social problem will affect the way we conceive of its solution. If we have an incomplete definition of a problem, then we will envision a limited solution. If the real problem is larger than our restricted definition, then our solution will be insufficient.

Years ago I was watching a daytime talk show which focused on interracial romantic relationships. On this show, the father of a white woman did not approve of his daughter's engagement to a black man. Yet when members of the audience called him a racist, he objected. From his point of view he was not a racist because even though he did not like blacks, he would not use the *n* word. Because he defined a racist as a person who used a particular racial insult, he felt free from the charge of racism. His limited definition of *racist* (voicing racial epithets) led to a limited solution (only avoid saying racial epithets). He was blind to the pain that his attitude caused both his daughter and the man to whom she was engaged.

If we are honest, we will admit that we also tend to define racism in a way that allows us to escape blame or to gain social resources from others. The father on the talk show may differ from us in degree of hypocrisy, but not in the effort with which we seek self-serving definitions to excuse ourselves. By our manipulation of words, we try to define away our own sins.

There are two dominant ways in which people in the United States define racism: the individualist definition and the structuralist definition.

AN INDIVIDUALIST DEFINITION OF RACISM

An individualist understanding defines racism as something overt that can be done only by one individual to another. This definition relies on the concept of freewill individualism, in which ultimate responsibility lies with the choices that human beings make. This philosophy assumes that individuals have the capacity to choose right from wrong and that sin is the result of our wrong choices. Society's problems rise from the sins of individuals. For example, the wrong sexual choices of many people have led to the spread of suffering and death from AIDS.

The individualist definition of racism holds that racial strife is the result of individuals choosing to act in a racist manner. If an apartment manager decides not to rent an apartment to a black applicant, then that manager is guilty of the sin of racism. If a teacher uses an insulting racial epithet against Hispanics, then the students will suffer from a racist action. If a personnel officer refuses to hire an Asian applicant, that is another example of racism. Christians who accept an individualistic definition of racism perceive these choices as sinful, and they perceive the effect of these sinful actions as racism.

Important work done by Michael Emerson and Christian Smith indicates that white evangelicals are more likely than other whites to adopt an individualist concept of racism because they have such a strong concept of personal sin.[1] The white racist is seen as a sinner who must repent of his or her sin. It does not take a great leap in logic to understand that if all people are capable of racism, then people of color who discriminate against majority group members are also guilty. People of color may be guilty of other sins connected with racial problems. For example, African Americans are less likely than European Americans to sustain intact families, a fact which contributes to their lower economic status.[2] From an individualist point of view, racial economic disparity can be the result of the sins of African Americans.

If the problem of racism is due to the individual shortcomings of racists, then the solution to racism lies within the individual. If we can eliminate the tendency of individuals to engage in racism, then we will eradicate any mistreatment of people based on race. Laws can play a part in the solution only so long as they mandate that individuals will be treated equally. Teaching people about the evils of racism can also be a solution, since we will learn how to treat each other in an egalitarian manner. Whether by law or teaching, this view locates the problem of racism within the individual; the solution is to help individuals overcome the personal racism in their hearts.

A STRUCTURALIST DEFINITION OF RACISM

In contrast to the individualist definition of racism is the structuralist definition. According to this view, society can perpetuate racism even when individuals in the society do not intend to be racist. The structuralist viewpoint rests on the idea that humans are affected by the social structures in which they live. People do not merely make personal choices; they make choices influenced by the structures of their society. Merely exhorting weak-willed individuals to stop sinning will not solve racism; our social structures must also be reformed.

For example, black and Latino youths tend not to do as well academically as majority group members.[3] Advocates of structuralism would argue that the difference has nothing to do with the students' innate abilities. They would say that the disparity exists because black and Latino students attend schools that are inferior to predominantly white schools. The structualist explanation does not necessarily blame overt white racism for the poor schools but instead finds fault with the insufficient funding that the schools receive. Public schools are funded largely through property taxes. Through these property taxes, wealthy people pour more money into their children's schools than poorer people are able to do. Personal racism is not to blame for the poor education of people of color; we should blame the social structures by which schools are funded.

The downplaying of individual blame is an important part of the structuralist view of racism. Those with a structuralist view do not dismiss the evidence that overt racism still plays a role in some racial problems. However, they assert that racism can affect the life prospects of people of color even when majority group members do not intend to act in a racist manner. The structuralist viewpoint sets forth an expanded definition of racism which includes acts of personal racism but also goes beyond them to include the way racism plays itself out in social structures. Since structuralists no longer need to prove ill will on the part of the majority, they are free to examine how social structures solidify racial inequality even when people do not overtly support such racism.

Emerson and Smith also note that African American evangelicals are more likely than other blacks to hold a structuralist viewpoint.[4] We can attribute this tendency to black people's desire to define racism in a way that will aid people of color. If blacks and other people of color include social structures as an aspect of racism, then they are more able to demand that society change those structures. Since racial minority groups have less than average income and wealth, they are motivated to push for social changes which will bring more economic equality. Obviously social reforms that concentrate on producing economic equality will lead to policies such as affirmative action, which work to the benefit of racial minorities. Structuralists may differ among themselves about how best to help people of color, but they agree that an alteration of social structures is part of the solution.

I want to make one final observation about these two basic definitions of racism. Emerson and Smith observed that blacks are more likely than whites to be structuralists.[5] But, as noted above, white evangelicals are even more individualistic than other whites, and black evangelicals are even more structuralist than other blacks. In other words, in their ideas about how to solve racial problems, white and black evangelicals are even farther apart than whites and blacks in general. How can it be that white and black evangelicals, who largely share the same theological beliefs, have such divergent views about racial issues? It is vital that we begin to explore a common faith-based way to tackle racism, if for no other reason than to enable us to pull together Christians of different races into a truly unified body of Christ and present to the world a witness worthy of our Lord.

DIFFERENT DEFINITIONS, DIFFERENT SOLUTIONS

Individualists do not understand why fixing racist structures in society is so important because they do not believe that racism is found in social structures. Likewise structuralists cannot understand how individualists can fail to see the problem with structures, and they believe that individualists are insensitive to the real issues of racial inequality.

Both the structuralist and the individualist definitions ignore the spiritual dimensions of racism. They are secular definitions. Neither definition speaks to the nature of humanity or to spiritual forces that transcend individuals and society. Christians should not be limited to thinking only about the spiritual dimensions of racism, but racism must ultimately be defined as a result of our human sin nature. The sin nature of both majority and minority group members leads to racial conflict and tensions. We cannot end racism until we confront our own sin nature.

THE ROLE OF OUR SIN NATURE

It is easy to get swept up in all the statistics, arguments and calculations which surround racial issues in the United States. Sometimes it is useful for us to step back and take a simple look at a complex problem.

For centuries certain racial groups have been abused by a racial group that has enjoyed a lot of power. Recently our society has seen the error of its ways and has granted those abused individuals equal legal and political rights. However, the granting of such rights has not wiped out the effects of centuries of abuse. Estranged relationships between those who have been in power and those who have been abused do not heal merely because we have passed certain egalitarian laws. There must be an intentional effort at racial healing.

So what do we do now? The groups who have benefited from historical abuse tend to want everyone to forget about the past and move on. The groups who have been historically abused tend to want to focus on historical evils and gain recompense for the wrongs done to them. In a nutshell this is the source of our contemporary racial conflict.

Such a simplification is useful because we can clearly see our sin nature in our own reactions to past events. Our sin nature seeks to be released from all measures of accountability. It is in the interest of whites to ignore the perspective of people of color and to minimize their concerns about racial justice. If whites take seriously the effects of historical and contemporary racism, then they will have to take measures to eliminate or at least limit those effects. The power and influence of the majority can only be diminished, since they already possess disproportionate amounts of power and status. I do not mean that all European Americans are well off and all racial minorities are poor, but in general whites have more social resources than racial minorities. If we assume that racial groups do not differ in intelligence, work ethic or other aspects of human ability, then we must assume that something in contemporary society and/or from our racist past accounts for these economic differences. Defining racism in an individualist manner can help majority group members maintain their advantages. Thus the individualism of European Americans is at least somewhat connected to their own sin nature and desire to ignore the plight of people of color.

Likewise it is in the interest of people of color to focus on historical and contemporary racism to explain the current state of our society. We do not have a history of systematic oppression of whites by people of color. Nor is there evidence today that our society is set up for the benefit of people of color. Concentrating on historical and modern forms of institutional racism can insure that responsibility for all racial problems will ultimately be placed at the feet of European Americans. Of course this approach absolves people of color of accountability for their own shortcomings. Thus we see a powerful tendency in some social and academic circles to deny the ways that people of color victimize each other and even majority group members.

But cannot the two sides see how their perspectives affect each other? Cannot whites perceive that their unwillingness to take seriously the disadvantages of people of color only alienates them from racial minorities? Cannot people of color understand that contemporary whites should not forever bear the guilt of the sins of their ancestors, and that their own sins contribute to the difficulties of their lives? Neither group will be able to recognize its own part in our racial problems until we acknowledge how our sin nature contributes to those problems. It is the very essence of our sin nature that so often causes the truth to be hidden from us. Mark McMinn, a Christian psychologist, rightly points out that humans have a natural tendency to see others as sinners and wrong, while we see ourselves as right.[6] If we get into an argument with a friend or spouse, we cannot understand how the other person cannot see our viewpoint. Our sin nature generates pride, which makes us unable to see how we have contributed to the problem. It is always someone else's fault.

Now we can understand why whites and people of color do not easily perceive each other's points of view. We can understand why whites emphasize individualism while people of color emphasize structuralism. Our sin nature keeps us from recognizing our own shortcomings. Instead we focus on what others should do. The group who has benefited from the ravages of racism fails to recognize those ravages, since it would mean they must accept a level of accountability they do not want to accept.[7] The groups who have been abused fail to recognize how things have gotten better and the fact that not all their problems can be blamed on racism. If we define racial problems in a way that does not include recognition of our sin nature, then we will have an incomplete definition and will be able to offer only incomplete answers.

USING MODELS TO UNDERSTAND POPULAR RACIAL SOLUTIONS

From the two secular definitions of racism there have been four general paths that Americans have taken. These four models generally represent the secular racial solutions found in the United States. Christians latched onto these solutions and came up with the more spiritualized term *racial reconciliation*.[8] Our attempts at spiritualization are admirable, but they cannot hide the fact that we have generally taken secular concepts and given them a Christian makeover. We should avoid making the mistake of thinking that just because we have spiritualized a secular model, the model is any less incomplete.

I want to be clear that I make no judgment about the sincerity of those who advocate different models. I believe that most of the proponents of these models honestly want to end the racial problems in our society and truly believe that the model they support is the best way to deal with racial problems. Yet sincerity is not sufficient for finding a solution to racism.

All of us are biased, and it is our natural tendency to see only the strengths of the models that we favor and the weaknesses of the models we do not like. It is quite difficult to see the advantages of models we hate and the shortcomings of those we love. But if Christians are going to find a better solution than the current secular models, then we have to be honest. We have to be as honest about the weaknesses of the model we love as we are about the model we hate. So the next step in the process of finding a Christian solution to racial problems is to gain a more complete understanding of the current secular models and to know why they sometimes succeed as well as why they ultimately fail.

FOUR MODELS OF RACIAL RECONCILIATION

The first model is *colorblindness*. Proponents of the colorblindness model argue that we will have racial reconciliation once we ignore race and forget the discrimination of the past. They contend that by concentrating on the advances we have made and acting in a colorblind manner we can overcome racism. The second possible model of racial reconciliation is *Anglo-conformity*. With the Anglo-conformity model, racial minorities are encouraged to adopt European American values so that minorities will imitate how whites moved up the economic/social ladder. Once racial minorities have gained economic equality with majority group members, then we will be able to overcome racism. Both the colorblind model and the Anglo-conformity model are based on the idea of individualistic racism.

The other two models focus on structural racial issues. The model of *multiculturalism* deals with racial alienation by emphasizing the value and worth of minority cultures. Advocates of this model argue that because the dominant society holds racial minorities and their subcultures in low esteem, we must find ways to uplift minority individuals and cultures. The final model, that of *white responsibility,* locates racial problems completely within majority culture and individuals. Its advocates argue that racial minorities cannot be racist since they lack the economic and social power of whites. Solutions that emerge from the white responsibility model tend to revolve around the empowerment of racial minorities.

In the following four chapters I will flesh out the four secular models more fully, first by looking at their sources. After examining the strengths and weaknesses of each model, I will look at their Christian adaptations, then attempt a Christian critique of them. Only after we have examined the secular models will we be ready to delve into the Scriptures to explore a Christian solution to racism.

2

Colorblindness

I suspect that colorblindness is the most popular model for how to deal with racial issues in our society. It is clearly the preferred model of politically conservative and even moderate majority group members, and it has made significant inroads into nonblack racial minority communities. Several race and ethnicity researchers have invested a great deal of time exploring the foundations of the colorblindness model.[1] Some researchers even suspect that racism is at its roots.[2] As with all the other models, I will assume that its advocates have the best intentions of ending racial strife in the United States. Furthermore, it is not so much that this model, or any other model for that matter, is wrong, but that it is incomplete.

The core argument of the colorblindness model is simple: to end racism, we have to ignore racial reality. Laws concerning racial issues must aim for the completely equal treatment of people of all races.[3] Such equality means that we must outlaw old-fashioned racial discrimination of the Jim Crow type.[4] However, modern efforts to correct the historical effects of Jim Crow must also be curtailed if they include any component specific to one race, because if we emphasize racial issues, then we will continue to have racial problems.

Advocates of colorblindness contend that efforts to alleviate our economic racial divide only elevate the importance of race, which in turn only reinforces the negative power of race in our society. They say that if we only stop taking race into account, racism will lose its power to alienate people from each other. The aim is to get beyond racial issues. The colorblind vision is of a society in which racial features such as skin color and facial structure are no more important than height or hair color. Then there will be no judgments based on race because race will carry no social importance.

THE SECULAR ROOTS OF THE COLORBLINDNESS MODEL

Ironically, many proponents of the colorblindness model find justification in the development of the modern civil rights movement. The original push of the civil rights movement was to free African Americans, and eventually other racial minorities, from overt racism. The major target of early civil rights leaders was the Jim Crow system of oppression in the South. Martin Luther King and other early civil rights leaders attempted to win equal treatment for racial minorities. The core of King's methodology, nonviolent protest, was built on the assumption that when whites saw how badly people of color were treated, then they would help minorities achieve equal rights.[5]

From within the civil rights movement the seeds of colorblindness began to grow. As the movement gained influence, the ideology of white supremacy became less acceptable, and those who advocated overt racist ideas began to fall out of favor. The concept of equal treatment was accepted by mainstream American society. But equal treatment was not limited to how whites should treat racial minorities. Majority group members should also be able to live free from bias based on skin color. The result was the philosophy of colorblindness.

For example, David Horowitz has documented his involvement in the 1960s protest movements, including the civil rights movement.[6] Yet today he is best known for his attempt to put advertisements in college newspapers that many consider racist attacks on the idea of racial reparations. Horowitz argues that reparations are a form of reverse discrimination, which is unfair to nonblacks.

Horowitz's ads are clear examples of the concept of colorblindness. He argues that the civil rights movement has largely accomplished its goals and there is no longer any need for intentional attempts to improve the lives of racial minorities. His contention is that the 1960s protests were about colorblindness, and that should be the goal today as well.

Advocates of colorblindness spend a good deal of time talking about reverse discrimination. The basic assumption of colorblindness is that racism has largely been defeated. People such as Dinesh D'Souza,[7] Ward Connerly[8] and Stephan Thernstrom[9] contend that historical racism was a great evil, but we have conquered that evil. They believe that while some people still hold on to their personal racism, they are fewer and fewer. They argue that racial minorities now have the same chance at success as majority group members. If minorities have the same economic and legal opportunities as other people, then efforts to help them will give them an unfair advantage.

The implications of the colorblindness model are clear when we look at conservative political activism. The colorblindness model can clearly be seen in issues such as affirmative action and hate crimes legislation. Colorblindness proponents argue that affirmative action is unfair because it rewards members of certain groups solely for their racial status.[10] Awarding jobs and college placements because of race, even if race is only a part of the calculation, indirectly penalizes whites, who are left out of the process. Instead of factoring race into occupational and educational decisions, proponents of colorblindness argue for a meritocracy by which everyone is equally and fairly judged. Likewise, hate crime legislation is rejected because it ranks some crimes as worse than others merely because of the race of the victim, when race should have no bearing on how the victim or perpetrator is treated in our justice system.[11]

STRENGTHS OF THE COLORBLINDNESS MODEL

The colorblindness model sets up a laudable goal that, if reached, would undoubtedly remove racial problems from our society. If we can diminish the importance of race, then racial stratification and alienation will no longer be possible. The dysfunctional aspects of a racialized society gain their power from the value, good or bad, which we assign to members of distinct racial groups. For example, we historically placed a high value on the possession of the phenotypical qualities of those we call *white*. People who exhibited those qualities were given more formal and informal social and political rights than people who did not have those qualities. However, today there are race-specific economic and educational programs which reward those who have the phenotypical characteristics associated with being black, Hispanic or Indian, while they deny benefits to those with phenotypical characteristics associated with being white or Asian. Being white is then associated with a negative value while certain other groups are given a positive value.

While many people agree that it is important to correct past racial injustices, the attempt reinforces the importance of race and continues the practice of assigning positive or negative values to different racial groups. Once we are content to rely on the valuing of one race over another as a solution to racism, how can we be sure that those who seek this justice—racial minorities—will ever be satisfied with the outcome?[12] Will they not have the incentive to maintain an unfair system as long as it is unfairly working for them? Such groups would have no reason to remove affirmative action programs even after they have achieved a level playing field with the majority.

This leads to a second strength of the colorblindness model. Colorblindness helps us correct the tendency of some racial minorities to look for racism where it does not exist. Since having the status of a victim can lead to more power, people of color have an incentive to seek out victim status whenever they can find it. By accusing someone or some organization of being racist, people of color can make claims on that person or organization. If the accusations are made often and if at times they do not appear to have merit, how can we know whether to act on them or not? Colorblindness gives us criteria by which we can decide. If it can be shown that people of color are being treated differently from the majority, then we can assume there is racism and act accordingly. Short of such proof, the colorblindness perspective argues that we should look for reasons other than racism.

In fact the colorblindness model goes beyond challenging claims of racism. Advocates of this model contend that the acknowledgment of race actually contributes to racial strife. Only by removing the value that is placed on racial status can we ever hope to take away people's incentive to benefit from race-specific programs or practices. Only a culture that is prepared to remove any valuation on race can hope to cure racial strife once and for all. Thus the goal of colorblindness, a society in which race no longer matters, at least theoretically promises a society which is more fair than any we can create by artificial attempts to right past wrongs.

It is a mistake to take the laissez faire attitude of colorblindness and expand it to say that we should ignore racism. The drive for a colorblind society was one of the major forces behind the passing of modern civil rights legislation. The laws that prevent racial minorities from facing the overt discrimination of the past are based on the idea that no individual should be mistreated because of racial status. Such legislation has opened up many previously forbidden social, economic, educational and political realms to people of color.

A classic example is the removal of laws against interracial marriage. Rachel Moran argues in her examination of the legal history behind interracial marriage that the Supreme Court utilized a colorblind analysis in order to justify throwing out those laws.[13] The Court argued that no government entity had a right to use race as a reason why people could not choose a marital partner. When it came to the marital choice of individuals, the government had to be colorblind. Advocates of colorblindness can argue that their racial philosophy is capable of creating all the legal regulation necessary to guarantee that racial minorities get a fair social environment. They can contend that legislation not based on a colorblindness model is likely to create an unfair world in which racial minorities are overcompensated for their racial status.

WEAKNESSES OF THE COLORBLINDNESS MODEL

For all its strengths, colorblindness is still an incomplete way to deal with issues of race. The colorblindness model has serious flaws. Its first weakness is that advocates of colorblindness are, at best, naive about their ability to deal with the historic effects of racism by pretending that race no longer matters. They tend to underestimate the lasting effects of historic racism.

Colorblindness assumes that the longer we live in a society where race is unimportant, the more surely racial inequities will fade. This is not realistic. Racial discrimination is deeply embedded in our society in many different ways, and only intentional and race-specific measures will remove its effects. For example, Douglas Massey and Nancy Denton's classic work on racial segregation indicates that segregation was not an accident but the result of deliberately racist policies.[14] Even after racist policies have been eliminated, segregation persists and the damage done by segregation remains. Ignoring the importance of race will not eliminate residential segregation. Since wheels were intentionally put into motion to create segregation, it will take other intentional efforts to end it.

Can anyone who understands the degree to which Native Americans lost their culture and resources ever believe that merely removing overt attempts at racism will allow Indians to gain economic equality with majority group members? On many reservations, Native Americans suffer from unemployment rates that approach 50 percent. There is no reason to believe that Indians as a group will be able to economically compete with members of other racial groups unless there are race-specific programs that allow them to do so. It is not realistic to believe that the colorblindness vision of equality is going to happen without some economic leveling between the different races, and this leveling is likely to require race-specific programs.

A second major shortcoming of the colorblindness model is that the attempt to ignore race leads to distortions which actually perpetuate racial strife. For example, members of many racial minorities have written eloquently about the pain they suffer because of their racial status.[15] Advocates of colorblindness tend to ignore this pain. The pain will not go away merely because it is ignored. It will only be submerged and passed on to future generations, or it will come out in violence and bitterness. The model of colorblindness has no answer for how to help minorities deal with the pain of racism. The only answer it provides, which is to minimize the importance of the pain, serves only to intensify the harm.

I remember listening to my grandmother talk about hiding from white supremacists when she was a child. Even though she had many white friends, I noticed that she never discussed these events when she was around European Americans. She talked about these things only with other African Americans. Most blacks who directly suffered at the hands of the Klan are now dead, but racism has scarred people of color in other ways that may inhibit their relations with majority group members. As Christians, are we to ignore such pain? Or are we to find ways to heal it? The colorblindness model offers us no way to heal the pain but only tells us to ignore it. This is less than what Christ would want.

Finally, while I do not want to question the integrity of advocates of colorblindness, there are those who do not really want an egalitarian society and who use the ideas behind this model to prevent racial equality. We would be naive not to recognize that some support the concept as a way for dominant group members to maintain their superior position.[16]

Since white supremacy is no longer acceptable, the next best way European Americans can cement their racial advantages is by advocating colorblindness.

Even if advocates of colorblindness can end all racial validation, we must recognize that the life prospects of members of different racial groups differ widely. Despite the assertions of reverse discrimination, majority group members still have advantages over racial minorities. We need only look at the percentage of whites in the highest positions in government,[17] the military[18] and business[19] to see that whites as a group have more social benefits than members of other racial groups. Given such a social reality, those who fight to maintain the racial status quo are in fact working to insure that whites remain in the top position of the racial hierarchy. The philosophy of colorblindness gives advocates justification to ignore the concerns of people of color even while claiming to work for a more racially egalitarian society.[20]

CHRISTIAN ACCEPTANCE OF THE COLORBLINDNESS MODEL

Even though it has a secular basis, the influence of the colorblindness model has reached into the Christian community. There are important similarities between the secular colorblindness model and the version Christians have constructed. Both versions of colorblindness are anchored in political conservatism. We see evidence of Christian colorblindness in the work of politically active conservative Christians. Like their secular counterparts, Christian advocates of colorblindness begin their defense from the modern civil rights movement. William Bennett, one of the strongest advocates of Christian colorblindness, openly talks about his activism in the early civil rights movement.[21] However, after his activism, Bennett went on to decry what he and Terry Eastland called *numerical equality* as opposed to *moral equality*.[22] The core of their argument is that we all should be treated equally regardless of race. They go on to argue that race-based programs that help racial minorities should be opposed as well as racist measures that deprive racial minorities of their rights.

I wish there were more older white Christians like Bennett who can claim to have taken part in the civil rights movement. In fact white Christians tended to try to slow down the civil rights movement or even resist it altogether.[23] Regardless of how badly Christians behaved during that turbulent time, contemporary Christians generally recognize the evils of slavery and racism. Those who perceive these evils through the lens of colorblindness believe, like Bennett, that we have largely conquered racism and do not need to make any more overt efforts to overcome it.

Many white Christians link their religious ideas to certain political ideals.[24] They have accepted the use of the colorblindness model to attack political policies such as affirmative action. Some white Christians have also attempted to add religious justification for colorblindness by pointing to Martin Luther King's famous "I Have a Dream" speech, especially as he said that he wanted his children to be judged by the content of their character instead of the color of their skin.[25] White Christian advocates of colorblindness are able to link their philosophy to the ideas of a famous black Christian pastor.[26] The most honest of these advocates admit that most white Christians were on the wrong side of the historic civil rights struggle.[27] But they go on to argue that today we must have the goal of nullifying the importance of race. In this way even Christians who did not fight for racial equality can still claim the high moral ground by arguing that they also strive for racial equality. They even argue that race-based solutions worsen race relations while the colorblindness model is the best way to improve race relations in the long run.[28]

World magazine is a major forum for politically active conservative Christians. In my experience, Christians with a colorblindness perspective generally do not like to discuss racial issues within an overtly religious setting because drawing attention to racial issues makes race more important. If Christians discuss political issues in religious venues, they are more likely to be conventional moral issues such as abortion or homosexuality.[29] *World* magazine is one outlet where Christians address more worldly issues.

An examination of *World* magazine reveals several articles from the colorblindness perspective. In one such article, Presca Shrewsbury, an African American, argues that she does not want to be judged by her racial identity but by her personal accomplishments.[30] She contends that race-based programs discount the ability of people of color to achieve on their own. Solutions to racism should rest on the ability of people of color to compete on an equal, but not superior, playing field with whites. Clearly Shrewsbury writes from the colorblindness model.

Another article in *World* magazine attacks the affirmative action program in Austin, Texas, as unfair. A black vendor refused to register himself as a minority business enterprise and lost out on potential business dealings because of his refusal. The writer criticized affirmative action because it does not allow blacks to succeed or fail on their own; it is even called "economic and intellectual slavery."[31] The argument implies that blacks become dependent on affirmative action to give them an advantage over whites, and they do not develop the resources to compete with whites.

In the world envisioned by colorblindness proponents, people of different races will be able to compete against each other, and the best person will get the job. This philosophy is generally identical to conservative political ideology. The writers in *World* magazine generally do not offer up much scriptural support for their positions.

I am not limited to *World* magazine to find examples of colorblind Christianity. Some articles in more explicitly Christian publications support colorblindness. Take, for example, an editorial by David Neff in *Christianity Today*.[32] Neff argues that in the wake of proposition 209 in California, affirmative action may be losing its political support. This does not bother him since he sees affirmative action as a creator of injustice. He argues that it may have had value in the 1960s but now it has run its course. He implies that only by moving toward a more colorblind society will we be able to advance toward real racial reconciliation.

A CRITIQUE OF CHRISTIAN COLORBLINDNESS

As we have seen, colorblindness is a secular philosophy built on worldly concepts of fairness. It is significant that Christian advocates of color-blindness do not rely heavily on specific Scriptures to support their position. This does not mean that colorblindness is devoid of any biblical support. Human equality is a powerful Christian value. One of the first lessons many Christians learn after conversion is that under Christ all of us have equal standing. Christ came down to die for all (Luke 3:6), and all of us are sinners before God (Romans 3:23). All of us need the blood of Christ to find salvation. Our race, sex or nationality has nothing to do with our position before God. Several times Jesus demonstrated the universality of his work by reaching out beyond the Jewish people (Mark 8:27-30; Luke 9:51-56; John 4:1-42). Faith in Christ was not to be limited by the ethnic boundaries of the time. Christianity is a religion in which superficial qualities such as a person's race become unimportant when we are confronted with the eternal significance of Christ. From an eternal perspective, it is definitely Christian to use the colorblindness model.

Yet while there is truth in colorblindness, it is still an incomplete model. It is built on individualistic ideas of sin. The Christian advocates of this model often do not address the structural aspects of racism. As I documented earlier in this chapter, many Christian advocates of color-blindness reject any social programs based on race. By doing so they ignore our society's structural racism. Sin is not only individualistic; a society can also suffer from structural sin.

In the Bible we find examples of leaders who attacked institutional sins. Nehemiah railed against the usury which kept people poor and in slavery (Nehemiah 5:6-11). James decried the unfair treatment of laborers by the wealthy (James 5:1-6). Amos condemned those who imposed heavy rents on the poor (Amos 5:11). In every case the condemned practice was legal but immoral. Institutional practices can be sinful if they punish society's unfortunate ones.

The colorblindness model is powerful in its call for a society in which race is no longer important. However, in its call to ignore racial issues, we find the seeds of its own failings. Ignorance of racial issues can spread to ignorance of the pain of minority group members and the need for race-specific solutions. While the colorblindness model aims at a laudable goal, it is naive in its assumptions of our ability to ignore race.

Colorblindness cannot offer a uniquely Christian solution for racism. A model which takes more seriously the idea that race impacts our lives is Anglo-conformity, the subject of the next chapter.

3

Anglo-Conformity

The Anglo-conformity model for dealing with racial issues is popular among majority group members and among minority group members of higher socioeconomic status. It finds support with people who are committed to American capitalism and who see economic inequality as the source of racism. If racial groups can obtain relative economic equality, then conflict between them will lessen or even disappear. Proponents of Anglo-conformity want to help members of minority groups achieve economic success.

The Anglo-conformity model overlaps with the colorblindness model in its assumption that minorities' lack of success cannot be blamed on contemporary racism. Minority group members can be successful if they work hard enough and are smart enough.

The Anglo-conformity model differs from colorblindness in its recognition that historic racism has inhibited minorities' ability to succeed, and therefore extra effort must be expended to overcome the effects of racism. This model does not automatically assume that our society is fair. Advocates of Anglo-conformity are strongly proactive. They assign responsibilities to both majority and minority group members. The majority must teach people of color how to succeed, while the minority is responsible for taking those lessons to heart so they can achieve economic and educational success.

Anglo-conformity is a very materialistic model. At its core is the belief that the real source of racial strife is economic disparity between the racial majority and minorities. Poverty, not overt racism, is the culprit. Economic disparity promotes negative stereotypes of racial minorities. Poverty leads to a higher level of crime and illiteracy in minority communities. Economic differences are also linked to residential, educational and occupational racial segregation. If we help racial minorities achieve economically, their success will remove their social stigma and lead to more complete racial integration and a more harmonious society.

ORIGIN OF THE ANGLO-CONFORMITY MODEL

The origin of the Anglo-conformity model can be found in the famous Moynihan Report of 1965. Daniel P. Moynihan, a former U.S. senator and sociologist, argued that slavery and racial oppression had created significant deficiencies in African American culture, leading particularly to the destruction of the black family.[1] This "tangle of pathology" within the black family led to other problems such as drug use, crime, lower income and out-of-wedlock births. As a solution, Moynihan proposed government programs in support of black families. By supporting African American families, society could rescue black subculture from the lasting effects of racial oppression.

We should ask why African Americans and Hispanic Americans remain at the bottom of many socioeconomic and educational measures while the economic fortunes of other racial groups such as Asians and Cubans in the United States have grown. In 1968 Stanley Elkins offered a possible explanation for the difference among African Americans. He argued that the brutality of American slavery made it impossible for blacks to develop their own social institutions. As a result, the cultural development of African American society was stunted and blacks were not able to develop the social structures that would help them to thrive.[2] Other researchers disputed Elkins's claim that the slavery of blacks was worse than other types of slavery[3] or that blacks were more submissive to the dominant group than were other racial minorities.[4] Yet the same argument has been made for Hispanic Americans. Oscar Lewis has argued that the deviant way of life[5] for Mexican Americans[6] and Puerto Ricans[7] has led to their continuing poverty. A culture that develops because of poverty continues to perpetuate poverty. We could also argue that Asians from Southeast Asia had their cultural development stunted in comparison with those from East Asia, which helps explain why East Asians achieve more success in the United States than do those from Southeast Asia.

The cultural inadequacy of racial minorities is not the only important feature of the Anglo-conformity model. William J. Wilson has argued that overt racism is no longer the main reason why African Americans fail.[8] He contends that class differences account for contemporary problems among blacks. According to Wilson, persistent discrimination and oppression led to the creation of a black underclass. The problem is not contemporary racism but stereotypes and discrimination against the poor. Theoretically, if economic inequality can be remedied, racial conflict will lessen and even disappear. The model of Anglo-conformity spurs the race versus class debate by insisting that class issues are more important than race issues.[9]

Hochschild applies her own take on Wilson's work with her assertion that there is a group of poor blacks who are so alienated from the dominant culture that they threaten the stability of African American communities.[10] She notes that most of the black poor still believe in hard work and the American dream, but continuing discrepancies between their ideals and their social realities threaten their beliefs. In that case the black underclass will endure until we can bolster the beliefs of poor African Americans and show them how they can succeed in our society.

Because the proponents of Anglo-conformity blame class issues for racial alienation, they tend to dismiss race-based programs such as affirmative action. They believe that if we have programs to help the poor, the programs should serve people of all races. Since racial minorities are more likely to be poor, people of color are more likely than whites to be helped by these programs. Supporters of Anglo-conformity advocate class-based rather than race-based programs. For example, since Asian and Cuban Americans have done well in our society, we do not need to pay as much attention to racism for those groups as we may have in the past. Instead we should teach people of color how to succeed, and their success will be the mechanism by which we overcome racism.

The solutions offered by proponents of Anglo-conformity are clearly tied to their definition of the problem. They believe that racial strife is created by economic inequality between the races. Historic racism created economic inequality because it produced a damaged minority subculture. To overcome economic inequality, we must reform the subcultures of racial minorities. Most Anglo-conformity advocates argue that it is the government's responsibility to create institutions that enable African Americans to succeed in a capitalistic society and to create stable families. This assertion is supported by the observation that other minority groups (Asians and Cuban Americans) who have been able to adapt to our capitalistic society and to maintain stable families have experienced economic success.[11] If racial minorities adopt the path of assimilation into European American culture, then we will be rid of racism.[12]

Advocates of the Anglo-conformity model ask why people who live in communities of color have been less likely to experience success. They argue that part of the explanation is ignorance about how to succeed in our society. Therefore they often attempt to train people of color how to succeed educationally and how to impress one's employer. People of color may also fail because they engage in practices that limit their own possibility of success, such as early childbearing. Supporters of Anglo-conformity try to find ways to change the cultural norms that lead to teenage pregnancy. People of color may not succeed because they do not have the social networks to land them the best jobs or place them in elite schools. Anglo-conformity supporters help people of color find the right social connections. In general, Anglo-conformists try to help people of color compete in the capitalistic American economy.

STRENGTHS OF THE ANGLO-CONFORMITY MODEL

Anglo-conformity has its attractions. It acknowledges that reducing economic disparity will lessen racial animosity. The lower socioeconomic status of people of color is one of the reasons for stereotypes that they are lazy or stupid. Lower socioeconomic status also leads people of color to resent majority group members.[13] People of color will perceive our society as more fair if they begin to share the economic success of the majority. Since capitalism is not likely to disappear anytime soon, racial minorities will benefit if they learn how to succeed by its rules.[14]

Another strength of the Anglo-conformity model is that it is more likely than other models to overcome economic disadvantages of racial minorities. Anglo-conformity is the model that gives most attention to economic concerns. If we pay no attention to how people of color are unable to compete in our economy, then we will fail to find ways to help them enjoy economic success.

Advocates of the Anglo-conformity model are practical about finding real solutions to the economic gap between majority and minority group members. They may acknowledge incidents of racism, but they prefer to focus on how to overcome its effects. Anglo-conformity resists promoting a fatalism which depresses the ability of minorities to overcome their problems. Because of their devotion to solutions, Anglo-conformists often perceive answers that others overlook.

A third strength of the Anglo-conformity model is that, while majority group members serve as advisers and mentors, they leave the key to solutions in the hands of the minorities. Anglo-conformists do not dwell on issues which racial minorities cannot control. Rather they focus on the ways that people of color can help themselves. They look for ways to give racial minorities the social and economic capital that carries the possibility of material success. They seek to empower lower-class people of color to be the source of the solution to their own economic distress.

While some may question the emphasis on the role of the minority, particularly those who envision the problem as the result of the excesses of the majority,[15] there is value in giving more responsibility to minority group members. If it is up to the majority to overcome our racial problems, then racial minorities are powerless to contribute anything to the struggle. At best the minority can only tell the majority what they should do and then hope that the majority is willing to own up to their duties. Anglo-conformity offers concrete ways for racial minorities to work toward their own economic emancipation. Anglo-conformity can empower racial minorities in ways that escape other models.

WEAKNESSES OF THE ANGLO-CONFORMITY MODEL

The truths of the Anglo-conformity model are offset by its inability to provide a complete answer for racism. The first weakness of the model is its shaky assumption that the greatest issues of racial strife rise from economic differences. It is true that people of color contribute to their own economic disenfranchisement. However, their failings do not happen in a vacuum. We must see the shortcomings of people of color in the framework of our society's prevalent structural racism. We cannot excuse racial minorities when they worsen their own economic situation through crime, teenage pregnancy or laziness; but these actions alone are not sufficient to account for the economic differences between the minority and the majority.

For example, research has indicated that much of the economic disparity between African Americans and majority group members is tied to residential segregation.[16] Blacks did not create this segregation. Research has shown that blacks are more willing to live next to whites than whites are willing to live next to blacks.[17] This unwillingness of whites persists regardless of the economic level of their black neighbors.[18] There is a visceral distaste that majority group members feel for African Americans, and the distaste is not limited to poor blacks.[19] Clearly racial animosity has social and cultural dimensions which are not tied to economic issues.

Another weakness of the Anglo-conformity approach is its assumption that the best way to achieve success in our society is through mechanisms rooted in European American culture. I do not imagine that Anglo-conformists have some evil desire to push European American culture on people of color, but it is a natural result of how this model developed. Because Anglo-conformist ideas are formulated by the majority, or by racial minorities trained by the majority, they naturally reflect the dominant culture. This tendency can lead Anglo-conformity advocates to miss out on other ideas.

For example, European American culture emphasizes individualism.[20] An emphasis on individualism can boost economic success, since it leads the individual to take responsibility for his or her own success and not rely on the efforts of others. For European Americans who live in a society that upholds their racial status, such an approach is very useful. However, individualism may not be the best way to insure the success of people of color. European Americans encourage their children to strike out on their own and create their own nuclear families. Separation from parents is a way that grown children prove themselves. However, many Asian immigrants find economic success through the cooperation of extended families. Their cultural norm is that children stay with their parents, and children and parents help each other, leading to a higher household income which benefits the entire family. Reliance on individualism would deprive these Asians from using their own cultural norms to further their economic success. Overreliance on the Anglo-conformist approach can lead to ignoring alternate pathways to economic success.

An unintentional consequence of individualism is the devaluation of the cultural perspectives of racial minorities, which is the third weakness of Anglo-conformity. Anglo-conformity implies that racial minorities are not successful because they fail to behave and work appropriately. Anglo-conformity winds up blaming the victim[21] by implying that racial minorities' own culture contributes to their economic failure.[22] As a result, European Americans can develop a savior complex toward people of color. It is not surprising that people of color complain about the paternalistic attitude of whites who are trying to help them.

Regardless of our racial identity, we all tend to be biased in favor of the way our culture does things. This tendency is not inherently evil. It can help us develop a healthy self-esteem. But it becomes a problem when we take our natural tendency and base universal imperatives on it. When that happens, what was only a cultural preference becomes a legalistic demand. We see a classic example in the early attempts by missionaries and social workers to aid Native Americans. Many Native American children were sent to boarding schools run by missionaries. At these schools, Christian Indian converts were compelled to cut their hair and wear European style clothing, demands based not on Scripture but on cultural taste. From these early missionaries and social workers we get the saying "Kill the Indian but save the man." The Eurocentric value of individualism also discouraged communal tribal living in favor of teaching Indians to be farmers, on the assumption that individualistic effort would help them compete in white society. The Anglo-conformist perspective can lead us to overvalue what European Americans offer and undervalue the priorities of racial minorities.

Finally, the Anglo-conformist approach is so tied to American capitalism that its supporters can become unable to comprehend noncapitalist solutions to racial alienation. From a neo-Marxian perspective, racial problems are the result of capitalism.[23] We saw in the fall of the Soviet Union that Marxism is not a panacea for our social ills. But to the degree that the problems of racial minorities are linked to capitalism, we may be able to learn some solutions from socialism and communism. For example, Marxists argue that capitalism perpetuates the economic advantages of the wealthy and their children.[24] Since whites have historically possessed more economic goods than people of color, then whites have a better ability to transfer their wealth to their children.[25] Anglo-conformists are unlikely to consider the possibility that capitalism may perpetuate our racial hierarchical system.

CHRISTIAN ANGLO-CONFORMITY

The Anglo-conformity model may be more attractive to Christians than to other Americans. The Christian worldview includes a strong concept of right versus wrong. The idea of a right path and a wrong path is consistent with the idea of the single path to godly truth (Matthew 7:13-14). We believe that those who find this truth find everlasting life. While this argument is usually made in theological terms,[26] it is an easy step for Christians to see it in cultural terms. Many Christians find it easy to assert that those who do not follow the proper cultural mandates are guilty of sin and must pay the consequences of their sin.[27]

Christianity can be used to strengthen the arguments for Anglo-conformity. For example, with Christian support one can claim that premarital sex and divorce produce both moral and economic consequences. From this perspective it is not only economically important to help people of color reform the ills of their culture; it is vital for their spiritual health as well. Moral laws apply to people of all races and all cultures. Christians are comfortable providing moral guidance, and if their guidance also leads to economic success, so much the better.[28]

A classic example of a Christian Anglo-conformist way of looking at racial issues is the autobiography of Star Parker.[29] Before her conversion she was a black unemployed single mother on welfare. After her conversion she started a local magazine business and eventually founded the Coalition on Urban Affairs, an "information clearinghouse on issues dealing with entrepreneurship, education, social policy for . . . pastors and businessmen."[30] For Parker the answer to the plight of African Americans is to help them leave the deviant welfare lifestyle and embrace entrepreneurship. She writes that dysfunctions within the African American family lead to dependence on welfare, which keeps blacks locked in the underclass. The result is that blacks look toward leaders who merely attempt to gain more government aid instead of urging blacks to work to achieve the American economic dream. Parker asserts that if blacks would put effort toward economic success, they would achieve it, and a major source of racial bitterness would evaporate.

Support for Anglo-conformity is especially prominent among Christians who work in an urban setting. Many Christian articles laud the work done by believers in poor communities.[31] Generally the recipients of help are people of color. The philosophy behind the help is a holistic Christianity which is concerned not only with the spiritual walk of the poor but with their economic situation as well. Wealthier Christians have an obligation to aid such people, even as the poor have an obligation to learn the skills necessary to help them succeed. From this point of view, occupational and educational skills are tools for evangelism as well as discipleship.

With the introduction of President George W. Bush's faith-based initiative, we are likely to see more efforts at Christian Anglo-conformity. Many of the organizations targeted by the faith-based initiative are led by people of color. It is an open secret that Bush hopes to use this faith-based emphasis to attract people of color to the Republican Party. It may prove to be a wise political move. The faith-based initiative has attracted a fair number of Christians. The model allows Christians of all races to work within communities of color in organizations that support their own religious beliefs and to receive governmental support for doing so.

A CRITIQUE OF CHRISTIAN ANGLO-CONFORMITY

In several places the Bible calls us to work toward economic success

(Proverbs 6:9-11; 14:23; Matthew 25:26-30; 2 Thessalonians 3:10). The Anglo-conformity model is right when it calls people of color to help themselves overcome their own economic problems. Our society often lives by situation ethics.[32] To the degree that Anglo-conformity reaffirms that there are right and wrong paths to morality, it can combat the consequences of situation ethics. It also reflects the Christian truth that sin has real consequences, and some of those consequences can be economic.[33]

But consequences and right versus wrong are only part of the story. The Anglo-conformity model fails, not because it recognizes right and wrong, but because it is an inadequate way to find the narrow path. When we factor in the cultural power of the majority, we see that the Anglo-conformity model allows a European American style of Christianity to become the dominant form of faith. It achieves dominance not because it is more biblically based but because whites who adhere to this style of Christianity have the most power.

Furthermore, the Christian Anglo-conformity model runs the risk of legalism. While we need to recognize right and wrong, it is easy to label cultural distinctives as sin when they are only different from our own culture.[34] Finally, as Christians we should ask whether it is biblical to base our answers on unconditional support of capitalism. The Bible warns against the sins associated with riches (Proverbs 11:4; Ecclesiastes 5:8-10; Amos 2:6-7; Luke 8:14; 1 Timothy 6:10; James 5:1-6). Wisely the Bible states that we cannot serve both God and money (Matthew 6:24). The materialistic emphasis of the Anglo-conformity model should be troubling to Christians.

CONCLUSION

Anglo-conformity allows us to address some of the important ways that our society hinders the economic advancement of racial minorities. This model has a helpful focus on economic empowerment. As long as we have powerful economic differences between racial groups, we have a basis for intergroup hostility. Yet this model's focus on materialistic concerns makes it an incomplete approach because it downplays the spiritual and moral dimensions of racism. It is unable to account for the noneconomic barriers that continue to hamper the efforts of racial minorities. Advocates of the Anglo-conformity model are vulnerable to charges of blaming the victim. Furthermore, this model projects an image of Eurocentrist arrogance, as it offers only European American methods of economic empowerment.

Anglo-conformity fits well with the Christian value of helping one's brother and sister. It is a model that calls for action, while the colorblindness model calls for mere acceptance of racial equality. Yet both Anglo-conformity and colorblindness rely on Eurocentric values. Unlike colorblindness, Anglo-conformity acknowledges possible structural racial effects.[35] However, Anglo-conformity depends on individualism; it focuses on empowering individual people of color to succeed. Given the prominence of individualism, it is not surprising that majority group members are more likely to support colorblindness or Anglo-conformity than the remaining two models of solving racial problems. In any case, Christian faith that is limited to European American cultural values cannot offer a complete solution to the social problems of racism.

Neither of the first two models takes seriously the potential abuse of power by the majority. They locate the source of most racial problems within communities of color rather than within the majority group. But if our racial problems are tied to a European American culture which benefits from racism, than both colorblindness and Anglo-conformity are inadequate models. They can never provide us with a unique Christian perspective on race.

The remaining two models offer a powerful critique of the Eurocentric nature of the first two approaches. In the next section, I will look at the first of these two critiques by examining multiculturalism.

4

Multiculturalism

Many white progressives and people of color have adopted the model of multiculturalism as the most promising way to solve racial conflict.[1] Multiculturalism can best be understood by looking at the philosophy of cultural pluralism,[2] "a situation in which each ethnic group preserves its own traditions, language, customs and lifestyle."[3] Multiculturalists want a society in which distinct racial and ethnic groups preserve their own identities. The larger society is theoretically constructed to insure that all racial and ethnic groups maintain economic and legal equality.

It is important to distinguish cultural pluralism from previous inegalitarian models of racial oppression (in which cultural separation was dictated to the minority by the majority) and from separatism (in which minority cultures separated themselves from the majority culture). Cultural pluralism allows minority cultures to establish cultural distinctiveness without any imposed segregation. In fact cultural pluralism cannot function if cultures are separated because economic equality is meaningful only if minority group members can interact with members of the majority group.

Multiculturalism is the practical application of cultural pluralism. Advocates of multiculturalism have written extensively about its implications for education,[4] the workplace[5] and other institutions.[6] They insist that minority cultures must be given prominence in order to offset centuries of dominance by European culture in North America. Since minority cultures have been devalued, there must be an intense effort to validate their worth.[7] Under multiculturalism, minority groups have a powerful motivation to resist assimilation into majority culture.

THE DEVELOPMENT OF MULTICULTURALISM IN THE UNITED STATES

Cultural pluralism as an ideology has its roots in the writings of Horace Kallen.[8] In 1915 Kallen attacked the idea that minority racial groups had to give up their cultural identity to be thoroughly American. He argued that members of all racial groups should be free to participate in all aspects of American institutions even as they maintain their own racial heritage. Kallen argued for the United States as a place where minority cultures are preserved and societal conformity is minimized.[9]

In the late 1960s and early 1970s, activists began to incorporate cultural pluralism into the educational system of the United States. They sought to expand American identity by lifting up the contributions of nonwhites and females.[10] Later multicultural activists moved away from assimilation or collective identity and toward the elevation of specific group identities.[11]

Education is now a crucial battleground for multiculturalists. The controversies over education are not limited to the inclusion of non-European courses; now they include questioning the amount of European-based courses offered, the development of bilingual curriculum and the incorporation of a multicultural perspective in nonmulticultural courses (for example, teaching Native American history in a U.S. history course).

Besides education, we see the influence of multiculturalism in public policies to encourage the use of different languages on official documents, in businesses that use culturally relevant messages to reach new American markets, and in diversity programs for social workers, police officers, health care deliverers, youth workers, supervisors, the military and others who must interact with various cultures. Multiculturalism is so pervasive that a former proponent of assimilation wrote a book titled *We Are All Multiculturalists Now.*[12]

No matter where we find multiculturalists, it is important to recognize where they lay the blame for racism: squarely on the majority's denial of the worth of nonwhite racial groups and their cultural norms. They see that the value of people of color has been denigrated while the worth of dominant group members has been overvalued. Multiculturalism tries to correct the injustice by promoting respect and appreciation for minority cultures and the contributions of people of color.

STRENGTHS OF THE MULTICULTURALIST MODEL

Multiculturalism promises to correct some of our society's Eurocentric excesses. Clearly there is evidence that European American influence is overly dominant.[13] Our language, holidays, style of dress and time orientation are all based on European culture. The strengths of non-European racial or ethnic groups, such as the communal and naturalist values of Native Americans, have been historically downplayed. Majority group members have gained an inflated view of their own importance while minority group members suffer from an undervaluation of their contributions.[14] For example, multiculturalists argue that whites and males are overrepresented in the literature taught in schools.[15] Good literature is defined as being from a Eurocentric perspective, while literature not written in a Eurocentric style is downgraded.

The dominance of European American culture makes it easier for people raised in that culture to succeed and to be validated by the academic canon. Majority group members enjoy advantages in other areas as well. Until very recently, we evaluated physical beauty by Eurocentric standards; the classic beauty had blond hair and blue eyes. We also tended to put a negative interpretation on non-European cultural practices; for example, the Hispanic siesta was seen as a sign of laziness.

Theoretically, multiculturalism will promote a society which focuses on the unique strengths of all its people groups.

Multiculturalism allows Americans to critique their own culture from the perspective of other racial or ethnic groups. If we learn to appreciate the strengths of people who are different from us, we will enhance our own lives and develop more respect for others. For example, we can learn the value of the cyclical perspective (rather than linear) found in Native American cultures or the respect for community seen in many Asian societies.

Earlier I stated that individualism is a hallmark of the European American outlook on life.[16] Grown children of European American families are generally encouraged to leave their family of origin as soon as possible. Majority group members often become isolated from other members of their immediate family. Other racial and ethnic groups avoid such isolation and enjoy benefits that escape European Americans. Research suggests that African American elderly are less likely to be depressed than European American elderly.[17] It is not unreasonable to assume that the lower incidence of depression is a result of the greater level of support that elderly of color receive from their extended families. While I have not seen research to substantiate it, I suspect that Asian and Hispanic elderly also enjoy benefits missed by European American elderly, since they command respect within their racial communities.

The final strength of multiculturalism is how it helps minority groups celebrate their own cultures. This is a great benefit because members of minority racial and ethnic groups have historically seen their cultures devalued. Multiculturalism helps minority group members favorably compare aspects of their own culture with aspects of majority culture.

Advocates of multiculturalism contend that an egalitarian society demands more than political and economic equality. Such a society also requires respect for all racial and ethnic groups. The colorblindness model envisions a society in which race is no longer a factor. The multiculturalist model envisions a society in which distinct racial and ethnic cultures are not only recognized but celebrated by all members of the society.

WEAKNESSES OF THE MULTICULTURALIST MODEL

Despite its strengths, the multiculturalist model has serious problems. While in theory it values all racial and ethnic groups, in reality its proponents denigrate the culture of the majority. Multiculturalists have positive things to say about racial minorities and are consistent critics of majority culture.[18] Perhaps supporters of multiculturalism must be critical of European American culture, since assimilation into this culture is their great fear. Yet we can reasonably argue that a society based only on African American, Hispanic American, Asian American or Native American values is no better than one based solely on European American values.[19]

With their criticism of the dominant culture, advocates of multiculturalism can unwittingly perpetuate the very actions they decry, the devaluation of cultures different from their own. In order to remain consistent to their principles, multiculturalists must find ways to raise the value of minority cultures without denigrating the value of the majority group. In theory this is possible. We do not have to belittle the majority to appreciate the minority. In practice, however, many of the most powerful advocates of multiculturalism have a postgraduate education built on a view of the world that endorses minority values and is very critical of majority values.

In their desire to enhance the perception of minority group cultures, multiculturalists tend to overlook minority shortcomings. They want to reverse the ways in which minority cultures have been devalued, yet in their efforts they sometimes err in the other direction. For example, several social observers argue that the actions of people in lower-class African American and Hispanic American communities contribute to their economic and educational failures.[20] Those who develop such an argument are often accused of "blaming the victim" and being insensitive to the difficulties of racial minorities.

A clear example of the problems which racial minorities can create for themselves is seen in the work of Laurence Steinberg.[21] Steinberg writes that African American students tend not to create a social environment supportive of academic endeavors. He points out the lack of academically focused peer groups among African and Hispanic American teens. As an African American who was an A student, I can attest that I lacked academic support from my peers. For my good grades they labeled me "Oreo" and "Uncle Tom," while white students in my school found support for their academic endeavors from their peers.

It is still true that structural issues must be addressed by those concerned about the educational success of racial minorities, but racial minority subcultures do create some of their own problems. Supporters of multiculturalism, who tend to blame black academic failure on the majority group, would likely resist such an assertion. If we are to solve the problem of black educational underachievement, then we have to be honest about all the sources of the problem, including any that come solely from choices in the black community.

The reluctance of multiculturalists to critique minority group cultures leads to another important weakness. Their unwillingness to critique makes it harder for multiculturalists to recognize universal social norms and laws. While multiculturalism may decry the use of universal norms, there is clearly a need for such norms. Some minority cultures have norms of gender, family, law, medicine, religion and diet that simply are not acceptable in our society. For example, some societies practice female genital mutilation.[22] The practice is based on deeply held moral and religious beliefs. Few proponents of multiculturalism would condone the practice, but the logic of multiculturalism makes it difficult for them to oppose it while supporting other controversial minority practices they want to endorse, such as the use of peyote. Multiculturalism often fails to create a proper balance between the need for cultural tolerance and the need to recognize absolutes which all of us must follow, regardless of our racial or ethnic group.

In Stan Gaede's critique of multiculturalism, he argues that while the approach has many positive features, its end goals are cooperation and harmony rather than truth and justice.[23] He contends that multiculturalism does not have the moral basis necessary to confront social and personal evil. Multiculturalists cannot promote truth because any assertion of truth is subject to whether it violates some cultural dictates of a given group. Instead of truth, we see relativism, the concept that all ideas and beliefs are equal.

It is my observation that in practice, multiculturalists do not live out their conviction that all ideas and beliefs are equal. Many are attempting to find ways to support the values which Gaede says they cannot support. Their philosophy makes it difficult for them to construct an ideological system to distinguish good from evil, since they avoid any concept of absolutes.[24]

MULTICULTURALISM AND CHRISTIANITY

In the last chapter I discussed how Christians may be susceptible to the ideas of Anglo-conformity because of their belief in right and wrong. We would expect Christians to be less likely to embrace multiculturalism because of its implied moral relativism. Yet our faith has always developed within a multicultural setting,[25] and there is a real danger of using the concept of absolutes to condemn cultural practices that are not sinful.

Christians who advocate some form of multiculturalism often find themselves defining it in a way that allows for the concept of right and wrong, while they try to discern the difference between what are truly Christian universals and what are merely cultural imperatives. Such a Christian perspective rises from Paul's argument against cultural legalism (Romans 14:1-6; 1 Corinthians 7:18-23) and his statement that he chose to become all things to all people (1 Corinthians 9:19-23). Multiculturalism finds a basis in Christian thought if it does not have to be reduced to cultural relativism.[26]

Christian multiculturalists resist the idea that Christianity must be based on European culture. They argue that it is a mistake to force people of color to assimilate into a Europeanized form of Christianity.[27] Instead they point out that allowing different cultures to develop their own expressions of Christianity enriches the faith of everyone.[28] Such enrichment helps us develop ways to reach out to people of different cultures and heal the pain of racism. They contend that we do not have to give up our core Christian beliefs, but we can find a new flexibility that will help us extend the kingdom of God.

Practical applications of Christian multiculturalism can be found in the work of Randy Woodley[29] and Clarence Shuler.[30] Woodley, a Native American Christian, discusses how the imposition of European Christianity damaged the ability of Christians to witness to American Indians. His critique of European Christians goes beyond their willingness to participate in oppression against Native people, such as genocide, forcing them onto reservations and stealing their land. He also criticizes the practices of well-meaning but misguided missionaries who taught European American culture as Christian culture. Missionaries forced Indian converts to give up their Native practices whether there was a scriptural basis for such a command or not. Woodley points out that this robbed Native Americans of their dignity. His ministry is contextualized, meaning that he operates within Native American culture in order to reach American Indians. He encourages Christian worship with Native American drums and clothing so that Native Americans can understand Christ in a culturally relevant manner.

Shuler's application of multiculturalism is a little different from Woodley's, but it is equally important. He maintains that majority group members must learn to listen to voices different from their own. Because whites have been trained within the dominant culture, it is easy for them to be insensitive to the concerns and ideals of people of color. Shuler encourages majority group members to listen and learn. He argues that white Christians should incorporate minority leadership into their ministries, and they must become open to solutions to racial issues which differ from their own preconceptions. Shuler does not focus on cultural alterations to the degree that Woodley does, but there is little doubt that European American Christians who take his advice seriously will become more accepting of cultures different from their own.

The essence of multicultural Christianity is that the lack of acceptance of non-Eurocentric Christianity has created barriers between Christians of different races. These barriers rob all believers of the ability to enjoy our faith in all its wonderful cultural expressions. Only when we tear down the barriers and learn how God is manifested in many different racial cultures will we come to true racial understanding. Past failures can be overcome if majority group members are willing to learn about racial minorities and if racial minorities are open to sharing their perspectives with white Christians.

A Critique of Christian Multiculturalism

The Bible was written in a multicultural context. Christian multiculturalists are right when they argue that we have a responsibility to avoid needlessly criticizing those who are culturally different from us. There are moral absolutes that are true in all cultures. But there is a powerful tendency to use the reality of absolutes to label as sin anything with which we disagree.

Many Christians do not realize that Paul's statement that "there is neither Jew nor Greek, slave nor free, male nor female" (Galatians 3:28) was directed at the Judaizers, Jewish Christians who tried to force all Christians to adopt cultural traditions such as circumcision. Paul's words were for Christians who wanted to force their practices on other Christians in issues with no eternal importance. We do well to listen to Christian multiculturalists as we try to balance the reality of absolutes with the need to refrain from arrogance about our own culture.

The problem with Christian multiculturalism is not that it is wrong but that it is inadequate to offer a complete Christian answer. We can understand that multiculturalists want to show the damage done by majority culture and that they want to uplift the culture of people of color. In light of the dominance of Eurocentrism, perhaps some of this emphasis is necessary for a time. But it leaves the impression, intended or not, that the culture of people of color is superior to that of majority group members.

Shuler spends a great deal of space in his book pointing out the failings of the dominant culture. When he speaks to the African American community, he tells blacks to keep speaking the truth, wait on God to help their white brothers and sisters, not let anger lead them into sin, and clean house on blacks who tell whites what they want to hear. Woodley also spends a great deal of time exposing the problems of the dominant culture. When addressing minorities he points out the failings of some Native Americans to support mixed bloods, urges them to forgive majority group members who repent of racial sins, and tells them to make sure they are not participating in our society's systems of inequality. In both cases, there is little in these books to challenge the cultural sins of African Americans and Native Americans, and little admission that the minority can benefit from majority group culture (although Woodley does show admiration for some of its technology). The reader is left with the impression that cultures of color have little or no sin, and majority group culture is nothing but sinful. In a future chapter I will discuss more of the consequences of minority group sin in an attempt to develop a more balanced Christian perspective on racial issues.

The model of multiculturalism fits the ability of our Christian faith to adapt to different cultures. However, the relativism inherent in this model makes it difficult for Christian multiculturalists to make an honest critique of minority group shortcomings. This difficulty shows the incomplete nature of a multiculturalist answer for racial problems. Only a uniquely Christian approach will take into account how our sin nature has damaged both majority and minority group members and their cultures.

CONCLUSION

Multiculturalism allows members of different racial groups to regain some of the esteem and honor that has been historically taken from them. It envisions a society in which all racial and ethnic cultures are valued. Christianity attempts to reach out to people of all cultures, and it is compatible with multiculturalism in its emphasis on acceptance of all people. Christian missionaries who sought out ways to share the gospel with those of different cultures can be regarded as some of the earliest multiculturalists.

Modern Christians have adapted many aspects of the secular multiculturalist model to try to create a Christian multiculturalism. The secular form of multiculturalism places such value on minority cultures that it promotes a relativism which ignores the sins in communities of color and makes it difficult to support universal norms to guide our society. Christians' adaptation of this model can reduce its harmful tendencies, yet the Christian expression of multiculturalism still delivers an imbalanced assessment of racism in the United States.

In an ideal world, multiculturalists would challenge European American culture but not criticize it any more than they criticize other cultures. Multiculturalists would merely point out that European American culture should not be the only one honored in our society. In reality, multiculturalists often place too much blame on majority group members and not enough responsibility on people of color. Yet there are those who argue that our racial problems have been caused solely by the shortcomings of European Americans. I call this perspective *white responsibility*, and I will examine it in the next chapter.

-- 5 --

White Responsibility

Perhaps the most controversial model for solving racial issues is what I will term *white responsibility*. This model receives support from both majority and minority group members who are highly critical of the social systems of the United States. Racial minorities, however, are more likely to support this model.

The core of the white responsibility model is that the dominant group creates problems of race and ethnicity. We might argue that the disappearance of overt racism is evidence that majority group members no longer have disproportionate racial power. But advocates of the white responsibility approach argue that majority social structures continue to victimize people of color. Like historic overt racism, subtle contemporary racism works to the benefit of the majority group. Therefore members of the majority have a social interest in maintaining the status quo.[1] Advocates of the white responsibility model contend that unless majority group members are willing to deal with the racism they create, the problem will not go away.

It is only fair to ask whether people of color have any responsibility to help Americans solve racial conflict. Advocates of white responsibility respond that people of color have limited, if any, responsibility for racial problems. In fact some assert that African Americans, and by extension other people of color, are unable to be racists.[2] From their viewpoint, racial minorities can have prejudice, but they cannot be racist because racism requires structural power. Since only dominant group members have structural power in our society, only dominant group members can practice racism.[3] European Americans are the ones who set up the social structures that perpetuate racism, so European Americans have the responsibility to remove these social structures. The only responsibility of racial minorities is to inform the majority group of the problems that their social structures create and to demand their destruction.

THE DEVELOPMENT OF THE WHITE RESPONSIBILITY MODEL

The white responsibility model has important intellectual origins. It emerged from ethnic studies programs that were an outgrowth of the civil rights movement.[4] As African, Latino, Asian and Native American students found a hostile environment in academia, they fought for their own separate spaces on college campuses. There, students and scholars from marginalized communities could assemble and articulate their goals for achieving cultural and political autonomy. As a result, 103 black studies programs and 100 Chicano studies programs were established by 1980. People of color began to shape an academic agenda that focused on the advancement of their concerns, safe from potential contamination by majority group influence.

Ethnic studies promoted the intellectual atmosphere that led to the creation of *critical race theory*, which holds that racism is an inherent part of American society.[5] Critical race theory argues that although the overt racism of white supremacy has receded, more insidious forms of institutional racism remain. Measures that appear to try to eradicate racism actually serve to perpetuate it because they deny that racism still has power. For example, recent court cases used the colorblindness model to strike down legal provisions such as affirmative action, which were created to help people of color overcome the effects of racism. The courts perpetuated the racial status quo, maintaining elite white advantage over racial minorities.

While a racist society lets elite whites keep their material dominance, it also shores up the self-esteem of lower-class and lower-middle-class whites. They may not reach the material level of the wealthier members of the majority, but they gain a psychological lift from belonging to the dominant racial group. Since the majority has so much to gain from racism, they will not willingly give up their power.

Proponents of white responsibility believe that our society must develop new arrangements for sharing power. Because racism is so pervasive, the new measures must take race into account. Majority group members would have to surrender excessive social power. There are various ideas of how the majority would transfer their power to the minority, but a commonly proposed method is through reparations.[6]

The argument for reparations is based on the assertion that the historic abuse suffered by racial minorities has impaired their ability to fairly compete in society. Because of this inequity, and because of broken promises given to certain minority groups,[7] proponents of reparations argue that racial minorities should receive some form of compensation from the majority. Reparations are a way for the majority to begin to correct the effects of the historic oppression of racism. In chapter eight I will look more closely at the argument for reparations and assess its value.

The white responsibility model lays the blame for racism squarely on European Americans and European American society. No one claims that all whites hate people of color. But regardless of whether a majority group member has personal racism, our social system works to the advantage of whites and to the disadvantage of people of color. For example, in a previous book I demonstrated how historic segregation continues to rob African Americans of their ability to receive the same quality of education as European Americans.[8] Because students attend schools mostly with people of their own race, more economic and social resources go to schools with majority group students. White responsibility adherents use such situations to point out that the problem is not personal racism but the more subtle racism of institutions.

The emphasis on institutional racism has led to the controversial claim that blacks and other racial minorities cannot be called *racist*. That is logical if *racism* means the effort by the majority to maintain economic and emotional advantages over the minority. Solutions offered by proponents of white responsibility aim to destroy institutions that exploit racial minorities for the benefit of the majority. Racial minorities have little role in solving the problem except to bring racial issues to the attention of whites who are willing to partner with them in the destruction of racist social structures.

STRENGTHS OF THE WHITE RESPONSIBILITY MODEL

The greatest strength of the white responsibility model is its ability to point out subtle ways in which the majority dominates society and perpetuates racism. While some people dismiss claims that racism still exists, advocates of white responsibility continue to offer evidence of majority advantage and proof that the minority still suffers from racism. An excellent example of such evidence is the concept of white privilege, first articulated by Peggy McIntosh.[9] Advocates of white responsibility use the concept of white privilege to show the subtle, and sometimes not so subtle, ways in which majority group members still benefit from their racial status.[10] McIntosh claims that she benefits from her racial status in many ways, such as being able to shop alone without being harassed, not being singled out by police or the IRS and not being expected to speak for all people of her race. White responsibility advocates point out that as long as majority group members continue to enjoy advantages, they will protect the racial status quo. Because few Americans want to openly participate in a racist social system,[11] contemporary racism is practiced in a manner which obscures its effects on the opportunities and freedoms of people of color. No reforms will be forthcoming if the majority does not perceive that there is a problem.

A second strength of the white responsibility model is that its proponents refuse to allow us to ignore our racial problems. We may not want to confront the ugliness of racism, but white responsibility activists constantly remind us that the issue is there. They will not let us be complacent about confronting individual, institutional and historic racism.

Advocates of the first two models, colorblindness and Anglo-conformity, tend to downplay the importance of racial problems. Even some who promote the multiculturalist model may hesitate to name the evil within European American culture, since multiculturalism takes a relativistic approach to cultural norms. However, as long as there are advocates of the white responsibility model, someone will always be calling racism to our attention. This is important because unless we acknowledge that racism still exists, we will not be able to remove its oppressive influences.

A final strength of the white responsibility model is that it helps remove some of the social stigma of belonging to a minority group. Some argue that people of color do not succeed economically and educationally because the surrounding society constantly tells them they are failures.[12] The perception of failure is reinforced by individualism, which holds that a person's success or failure is determined by the person's own effort.[13] It is not accurate to tie a person's success solely to his or her individual effort. Powerful institutional forces can aid or inhibit success, especially in a society as racialized as the United States.[14] White responsibility advocates remind people of color that talent and work alone do not determine success or failure. Prospects for success are affected by racialized social structures.[15] We can argue that until people of color realize how much the deck is stacked against them, they will not acknowledge how much they must overcome, and they may give up too easily.

WEAKNESSES OF THE WHITE RESPONSIBILITY MODEL

Despite its strengths, the white responsibility model has serious short-comings. First, it completely discounts the responsibility of racial minorities because it lays all the blame for our society's race problems on majority racism. Minority group members may at first find such a stance tempting. Being absolved of any responsibility, they can make demands on their white brothers and sisters while not having to worry about their own actions. On deeper reflection we see that such a position is actually disempowering for people of color. If they have no responsibility for our racial problems, then they are unable to play a significant role in reforming society. Racial minorities are forced to sit on the sidelines and wait for whites to put the proper reforms in place.

For example, some advocates of the white responsibility model claim that only whites can be racist. So while people of color can have prejudice, the responsibility of erasing racism lies with dominant group members. If Christians of color cannot be racist, then we can only try to help our white brothers and sisters overcome their own racism. If they accept our help, that is great. If they are not willing to accept our help, then we are helpless. By removing the responsibilities of people of color, the white responsibility model sets them up for increased frustration. No wonder there are so many angry minorities who advocate the white responsibility model. It is a philosophy that feeds the frustration deep within the soul of a person of color.

The second shortcoming of the white responsibility model is that it alienates whites who do not already feel a significant level of racial guilt. Because whites feel unfairly accused, they develop more distance from racial minorities. The white responsibility model does not help create harmony between whites and racial minorities. In my experience, whites rebel against the ideas of this model because they believe it is unfair to blame only majority group members. Defensiveness and anger do not make European Americans open to the possibility of racial dialogue and reconciliation.

White adherents of the white responsibility model do exist, both Christian and secular.[16] In my experience it is an all or nothing proposition for majority group members. Either whites totally accept the white responsibility model or they totally reject it as unfair. The vast majority of whites perceive it as unfair and reject it. It is unlikely that such a model will attract enough European American believers to build a strong multiracial consensus within the Christian community.

Finally, the white responsibility model is problematic because it ignores the fact that all people, including racial minorities, are sinners. The premise of the model is that only the sins of European Americans have contributed to racism. Whites can justifiably feel that they are being picked on unfairly. People of all races can and do engage in sin, even the sin of racism. All major racial groups have exploited other groups when they had power. An honest reading of history shows us that black Africans practiced slavery, that Native Americans brutally massacred each other before Europeans came to the New World and that some Asians oppressed other Asians based on ideas of ethnic superiority.

Supporters of the white responsibility model can respond that while all racial groups have the potential to engage in racism, in the United States it is the European Americans who have the power to consistently do so; therefore to delve into the faults of other racial groups will do little to help us overcome racial problems. I disagree with this argument. If we forget that people of color are also capable of selfishness and greed, then we fashion solutions which rely on people of color to exhibit extraordinary self-restraint. Even more than the multiculturalist model, adherents of white responsibility assume that racial minorities will not play the race card.[17] But because of the sin nature in all people, including people of color, it is likely that racial minorities will abuse the noble status given to them by adherents of this model. Racial minorities will seek advantages over whites whether those advantages are legitimate or not. The white responsibility model does not provide any way to restrain racial minorities from abusing their newly elevated position. A solution that leads to racial reconciliation must include ways to restrain both the minorities and the majority from promoting racial evil.

CHRISTIAN ADAPTATIONS OF WHITE RESPONSIBILITY

The Christian religion takes sin very seriously. How to deal with the consequences of sin is at the heart of how many of us understand our faith.[18] Our Christianity not only convicts us of sin but offers a solution by repentance and acceptance of the blood of Christ. The reason why many people refuse this free gift is that they fail to acknowledge sin's power to ruin us. To the degree that the white responsibility model is able to point out the sin of racism, it is compatible with a prophetic Christian call. Many conservative Christians limit themselves to an individualistic concept of sin. As I pointed out in chapter two, racism can manifest itself as structural as well as individualistic sin.[19] Because racism is almost universally recognized as sin, Christians who are sensitive to structural sin are likely to find some agreement with the white responsibility model. Once we go outside politically conservative Christian circles, we find a greater number of Christians who accept the white responsibility model.

Adherence to the white responsibility model does not require one to belong to a racial minority. One of the best-known Christian advocates of this model is a white man named Joseph Brandt. Brandt's book *Dismantling Racism* has become a key in his Crossroads ministry, which presents diversity seminars for Christian groups. Brandt begins with the basis that racism is a white problem because racism is not limited to prejudice by individuals; it is created by prejudice plus power. Brandt argues that because racial minorities lack power in our society, they do not have the ability to be racist. From Brandt's perspective, every white person is part of the problem because of his or her dominant group status. The gospel is needed to free whites from the prison of racism so they can participate in corporate action to tear down racism. Here we see two key elements of the white responsibility model: focus on the structural problems created by the dominant culture and the denial of minority group responsibilities.

Of course whites such as Brandt are not the only Christian advocates of white responsibility. One of the earliest calls for reparations occurred in a Christian setting when James Foreman announced at Riverside Church in New York that the churches and synagogues in the United States should pay African Americans $500 million as a beginning of the reparations due them. Since then, Christian groups have discussed whether and how reparations can be justified.[20]

Another avenue of Christian support for the white responsibility model is through what is called black theology.[21] Black theology is a Christian manifestation of a radical form of Afrocentrism. Black theology conceptualizes Jesus as black because Jesus represents the oppressed in society. Such an ideology allows blacks the leeway to do whatever is necessary to protest racism. Almost anything blacks do in the nature of protest is seen as furthering the work of Christ, because they are setting the oppressed free.

Another Christian manifestation of white responsibility is what is called liberation theology, which rose from Latin American Catholicism.[22] Liberation theology developed in response to the poverty of Latin American countries. It attempts to be a prophetic voice for the poor. Advocates of liberation theology contend that we find Christ in the struggles of the impoverished. Since liberation theology originated among Hispanic theologians and activists, racism is an important issue. Liberation theology is very critical of the capitalist system, and it presents socialism as the solution to the problems of race and poverty. Liberation theology can be seen as a Marxist Christian version of white responsibility. Although its roots are in Latin America, liberation theology addresses issues of global poverty in non-Hispanic nations as well. Both black theology and liberation theology have been criticized for not being scripturally based and for being generated purely out of cultures of color. The first criticism may have merit, but the argument of bias is flawed because it is doubtful that any racial solutions developed by human beings can be free from cultural bias.

More and more mainline churches are adopting a white responsibility approach to racism. It is not difficult to understand why this is happening, since elements of Christianity clearly support this model. Once the blame for racism is placed on European American culture, then a Christian concept of sin can be used to challenge that culture.

A CRITIQUE OF CHRISTIAN WHITE RESPONSIBILITY

The Christian adaptation of the white responsibility model correctly identifies the power of sin to create racial conflict. It is the nature of sin that we want to hide its effects. Christian advocates of white responsibility do not allow us to forget the awful effects of sin. They remind us that our society marginalizes people of color because of the personal and social sins of the majority. We can hope Christian white responsibility advocates can draw attention to these problems, which will help the church take racism seriously.

But the Christian adaptation of this model does not display any substantial difference from the secular version. The way Christian advocates of white responsibility apply their ideas about sin does not differ much from the methods of the model's secular proponents. Both aim to eliminate majority group advantage. Christian advocates of white responsibility are vulnerable to the same critiques as its secular adherents. For example, because Christian supporters of white responsibility focus on only the sins of the majority, they do not acknowledge how the sins of people of color contribute to racial conflict. White responsibility offers at best an incomplete blueprint for us to construct a satisfying solution for the sins of racism.

CONCLUSION

The white responsibility model comes in many variations. Proponents of this model can look at many sources of racism in European American culture. Westernized forms of capitalism, socialization, values and religion may all be culprits. However, this model will never be able to generate an honest dialogue between whites and nonwhites. The hostility which whites perceive from this model does not leave room for useful conversation. The emphasis on the sins of majority group members ignores the truth that all of us are sinners.

Understanding sin is at the core of our Christian faith. To the degree that the white responsibility model addresses sin, it is in keeping with Christianity. Yet Christian applications of this model do not enhance its prophetic ability, except to provide a sense of supernatural legitimization. Furthermore, this model's concentration on the sins of the majority leaves out important aspects of our Christian faith, including forgiveness and redemption. I will deal with those issues in the next chapter, because they must be part of any Christian response to racism.

None of the four models we have discussed is capable of providing a unique Christian answer for our racial problems. All of them are flawed because their secular philosophical origins limit their perspectives on reality. Beginning with the next chapter, I will map out a unique Christian solution that has the power to get at the root of racial problems in our society.

PART TWO

Finding a Christian Approach to Dealing with Racism

THE MUTUAL
RESPONSIBILITY MODEL

Toward Constructing a Christian
Solution to the Problem of Racism

Why have all the secular answers fallen short of solving our racial problems? More important, is there a Christian solution that can overcome the shortcomings of the non-Christian approaches? Does racial conflict have a spiritual dimension that compels us to look to our faith for remedies?

Secular approaches are adequate for some social problems. Learning how to organize the layout of a city does not require any special spiritual training. However, in other issues it is important that Christians contribute our unique perspective. For example, I believe that issues involving human joy require Christian insight. Through our faith we can find the eternal purpose and security that provides us with the foundation for joy.[1]

I believe that racism is a problem that requires specifically Christian insight. In this chapter I will begin to move from failed answers toward authentic solutions for our racial ills.

Human depravity, or sin nature, is a vital Christian concept which can help us deal with racial conflict. Most of us do not like to think or talk about it, but it is central to Christian belief. By understanding human depravity and how it affects racial issues, we can begin to understand why racial problems persist.

The problem of racism originated from human depravity. Human depravity makes us protective of our racial group's material interests, and it blinds us to other people's points of view. Human depravity is the spiritual dimension that keeps us racially separated.

In my attempt to find a Christian solution for racism, I am developing what I call a *mutual responsibility* model for racial reconciliation. It is a concept that takes seriously the Christian teaching of human depravity. Unlike the colorblindness and Anglo-conformity models, the mutual responsibility model does not ignore the historic and contemporary damage done to people of color by the majority. Unlike the multiculturalist and white responsibility models, it does not absolve minorities of responsibility.

With the mutual responsibility model, we look to Christian faith to overcome the effects of human depravity in race relations. We work to develop racial relationships based on our reconciliation with God.

THE FAILURE OF THE SECULAR MODELS

Before we can consider what a Christian solution looks like, we should consider why all the secular models have failed. On the surface the four secular models seem to have no similarity except that they do not rest on a biblical foundation. Yet there is a significant parallel between them. All four focus on a single explanation for why racism is a problem in our society.

In the colorblindness model, the source of the problem is our failure to recognize that race is unimportant. For Anglo-conformity proponents, the source of the problem is the inability of racial minorities to adjust to the majority economic and social system. Multiculturalism holds that the problem comes from the dominance of Eurocentric culture. For white responsibility advocates, the majority group is the problem.

Each of the four secular models identifies one source of racial conflict and proposes solutions to deal with that source. Certainly each source is at least partially responsible for racial alienation. The strength of these models lies in their recognition of a particular cause of racial tension and in their effort to solve it. Their weakness lies in their refusal to identify other sources of the problem. At best, these incomplete models can help us correct certain aspects of racial tension, but they will never eradicate the problem.

When I listen to the proponents of the four secular models, I always feel that I am getting an incomplete answer, even though I may agree with certain points. I generally go away feeling that the speaker is right in some ways but has not provided a sufficient solution. The sources of conflict they identify are real, but they are ultimately superficial. None of the models gets at the core of the problem.

The Bible teaches us that those who look at issues only through natural eyes will be unable to understand the spiritual dimensions of this world (1 Corinthians 2:14). If racial conflict has a spiritual foundation, then secular models are unable to identify the true source of the conflict. It remains for Christians to identify the foundation of all the sources of racial tension. If we fail to find this underlying source, we are doomed to limited and insufficient solutions for racism.

A competent medical doctor is not content to treat only symptoms. The doctor knows that the symptoms will return unless the cause of the symptoms is found and dealt with. When I have a fever, it is important that I get a lot of bed rest and apply cold cloths to my head. Doing so relieves some of the painful symptoms. But those measures by themselves do not heal me. I also need antibiotics to deal with the source of my illness. Likewise each of the secular models treats a symptom of racial estrangement. But all of them fail to locate the primary cause of our racial illness. Racism is a spiritual and moral problem. Only if we see how our sin nature is the primary source for all other sources of racial tension will we be able to stop treating symptoms and tear this disease out by its awful roots.

The mutual responsibility model takes our sin nature into account and puts obligations on both majority and minority group members, because the sins of both the majority and the minority contribute to racial tension. I do not mean that the obligations of both groups are identical. They are not. However, unless both the minority and the majority live by Christian principles, we are doomed to live alienated from each other.

HOW OUR SIN NATURE CAUSES RACIAL PROBLEMS

A core principle of Christian faith is the concept of the sin nature.[2] It is one of the defining ways in which Christianity differs from the other religions.[3] Our sin nature drives majority group members to look for both overt and subtle ways to maintain the advantages of their racial status. Our sin nature motivates people of color to use their victim status to gain whatever they can.[4] Our sin nature blinds us to the ways in which we protect the interests of our own racial group.[5] Our sin nature also influences us to blame others for the problems we cause ourselves.

The sin nature drives us to remake our images of God and society into what we want, blinding us to an accurate perception of society and God. Cornelius Plantinga contends that revised versions of God arise depending on who we want God to be.[6] Accordingly, many majority group members latch on to an individualistic definition of racism that relieves them of any responsibility for institutional and historic problems. They also focus on the shortcomings of people of color and overlook the ways the majority continues to benefit from the racial status quo. Plantinga argues that sin can be a masquerade by which we justify our self-deception. Furthermore, the sin nature creates selfishness which makes people of color expand their definition of racism to the point that they make inflated economic and social claims on the majority. They can then ignore their own responsibility and focus only on the responsibility of the majority group. Plantinga points out that those who perceive themselves as victims often fail to regulate themselves because of their sense of entitlement. How Christians define sin will determine how we try to solve social problems.[7]

The Christian doctrine of the sin nature rises from the belief that we are born in sin.[8] It does not mean we are unrelentingly evil creatures, but we are creatures who fail to obtain the moral heights that God wants for us. Our self-serving attitude is a part of us. We should not be surprised that the apostle Paul lamented his inability to escape the clutches of his own sin (Romans 7:14-25).

Charles Colson beautifully illustrates how our sin is part of who we are.[9] He quotes R. C. Sproul when he says that that we are not sinners because we sin, but rather we sin because we are sinners.[10] It is natural for us to be selfish and to look at how we can benefit from a given situation.[11] The doctrine of human depravity does not absolve us of responsibility to grow beyond our shortcomings, but it does confirm the reality of our shortcomings.

Plantinga maintains that the saddest aspect of sin is that it prevents what he calls *shalom*. *Shalom* is, in his words, *the way things ought to be*. Because of sin, the world is radically different from what God wants. Racial alienation is not what God wants; it is the natural consequence of our sin nature. The root of racial strife is not overemphasis on race, material inequity, the dominance of European American culture or the racism of majority group members. Those factors are significant, but ultimately our racial problems come from the sin nature that has invaded our souls.

The spiritual dimension provides a more complete and accurate definition of *racism* than either the individualist or structuralist concepts. Racism is a natural outflow of the racial divisions in our society as they are affected by our state of moral depravity. Clearly there are individualistic and structural elements, but at its heart, racism is spiritual. With this definition we see that only when we deal with our own moral depravity will we have any chance of ending the evil of racism.[12]

Once we accept that we are morally depraved, then we can find

Christ's gift of salvation. This truth is the central message of Christianity. Try as we may, we cannot even live up to our own standards.[13] I think that I am generally an honest person, yet I know that I am not 100-percent honest all the time. Even without the Bible, I would know that lying is wrong; yet I find myself lying anyway. I think of my lies as small lies that do not hurt anyone. I lie to make myself look good or to avoid a troublesome situation. The sin nature within me has morally trapped me into a lifestyle that I know is wrong. Only by coming to the perfection of Christ can I find the strength to begin to defeat the old self and to put on the new self (2 Corinthians 5:17; Ephesians 4:22-24; Colossians 3:9-10). No wonder Christian theology teaches us that we are in slavery to sin.[14] Even when we know we should act better, we often fail to do what is right. If a person understands the depth of his or her depravity and comes to Christ to overcome the sin nature, then that person understands the most vital truth of Christianity.

Salvation is the message which gives us the hope that we are not trapped in a life of sin. It teaches us the matchless love of Christ, who, being God, gave up all that deity had to offer to come and suffer so that we have access to the power that will ultimately free us from our sin nature (Philippians 2:6-11). Too often we do not consider any implications of salvation beyond our own spiritual well-being. We find individual freedom, but we do not recognize how our sin nature is the source of many social ills. We must consider how we can bring salvation to the social ills that plague us. The message of the Bible is not just that we are fallen but that God has made a way for us to recover from our fallen state.

OUR SIN NATURE AND RACIAL MISTRUST

Without an acknowledgment of our sin nature, we put too much faith in our own abilities. When we examine the secular models, another important similarity they all share is their overreliance on human ability and their underestimate of our fallen nature.

The colorblindness and Anglo-conformity models place great faith in the willingness of European Americans to either give up all their advantages for a truly egalitarian society (colorblindness) or help people of color gain an equal place in society (Anglo-conformity). It is reasonable for majority group members to prefer models which show trust in European Americans and call on racial minorities to solve their own problems. Since European Americans have had power for so long, and the record of how they have used their power is questionable at best and horrendous at worst, it is not surprising that people of color are not eager to trust them. European Americans, like all other humans, are trapped within their own sin nature, so racial minorities should not necessarily trust European Americans who are poisoned by their own human depravity.

Likewise the models of multiculturalism and white responsibility ask whites either to allow people of color nearly complete freedom to challenge all aspects of European culture (multiculturalism) or to allow people of color to set new power rules in society (white responsibility). Naturally racial minorities favor such models since they place the blame for racism solely on the majority. People of color may not have a history of abusing whites, but there is plenty of evidence that they are just as prone to abuse other humans when they have the chance. To appreciate this point we do not have to look only at black on black or Hispanic on Hispanic crime. When not painted over with a politically correct brush, the history of different racial groups reveals atrocities committed against other groups.[15] Furthermore, people of color have shown themselves willing to use their victim status to escape their own responsibilities. Whites do not trust people of color to unilaterally set up the new racial order. They should not trust us because we too possess the sin nature that makes us look out after our own interests, not the interests of others (Philippians 2:4).

Of course there are whites sensitive to the plight of racial minorities, and there are people of color who are careful not to dump unnecessary racial garbage on whites. There are always those exceptional individuals who bless us in this struggle with their ability to look beyond the interests of their own race. But our sin nature means that it is generally going to be hard for whites to understand the concerns of racial minorities as well as vice versa. Only by looking to the Christian concept of our sin nature and by embracing the concept of mutual responsibility can we tackle the core spiritual issue behind racism and hope to one day eradicate this social sin from our churches and society.

DEALING WITH OUR SIN NATURE

Human depravity means both good and bad news for racial conflict. The bad news is that all of us are sinners. If we are going to rely on our own human wisdom, we are doomed to make the same mistakes we made in the past. We are always going to have a strong affinity for solutions which help our racial group at the expense of other races. But there is also good news. By recognizing our sin nature, we can comprehend the spiritual dimension of our problems. Furthermore, Christianity has not only diagnosed the problem; it has offered the solution. The core of Christianity is about solving the fatal illness brought about by sin.[16] Our faith promises a day when God will empower us to free us from the slavery of our sin nature. By looking to our faith we can offer solutions with unique power to solve racial conflict.

Our faith has short-term and long-term implications for racism. In the long term we hope for the New Jerusalem, where old racial alienation will disappear forever. Only at that point will our restoration be complete. Then the sin of racism will be eradicated. Only at that point will we reach *shalom*.[17]

I know that I will not be sinless this side of the grave. Yet my faith can help me overcome my sin nature and grow closer to Christ. Likewise, we will probably never be able to completely eliminate racism from our society. Just as my sin nature will not totally disappear in my present physical life, the sin nature that is the source of our racial struggles is not going to completely go away.[18] But we can move closer to the moral perfection God wants. As Christians we are called to bring restoration where there was none before. It is our task as Christians to do all we can to heal our society while we wait for Christ's return, when we will see the end of all alienation and misunderstandings.[19]

I want to start what I hope will be an ongoing Christian dialogue about how our faith can help us deal with the sin nature that gives rise to our racial problems. I do not claim that I have arrived at the ultimate solution. Like everyone else, I too am infected with the sickness of my sin nature. I too have a bias to support my group over other racial groups. What I term the mutual responsibility model is not the final word, but I hope it is the beginning.

Mark McMinn writes that only by understanding sin can we hope to understand grace.[20] When we recognize the depth of our sin, we feel depressed over how depraved we are. We want to be free of the weight of our sins. McMinn points out how we attempt to erase our sense of sin through self-justification and explaining away our failures. Such attempts merely further the lies created by our sin nature and lead us nowhere. Only if we can be honest about our sin nature can we ever hope to overcome its corrosive effects.

But there is a risk that comes with acknowledging our sin. If we recognize that we sin or that we benefit from the sins of others, we give the victims of our sins tools to use against us.[21] They can use our confession to make demands on us. They can also choose to ignore their own responsibilities in our conflict. So instead of admitting our sins, we try to hide them from God and from others.

Here is precisely where the Christian concept of grace gives us the answers we need. We rely on grace when we confess our sins to God. We have confidence that God will not misuse our confession because he has proven through his matchless character that his love will not go away after we confess. But when we think of confessing to fallible humans, we cannot be certain that we will receive grace.[22] Our natural reluctance to confess is intensified by the possibility that those to whom we confess may make us pay.[23] So we lose the opportunity for grace to heal us.

If only we could be sure that others will offer us grace when we need it. Yet we have to look at grace from the point of view of the victim. Offering others grace is not without cost. We may fear that if we give grace too easily, we will forfeit our ability to make righteous demands against those who harmed us. Forgiveness becomes something we are hesitant to give.[24] We want those who sinned against us to acknowledge their sins and promise to provide true justice for us. Without their confession we are unwilling to mend our broken relationship with the majority group. We withhold our forgiveness so we can maintain our power over those who have wronged us, avoiding any admission of wrongs we have done to them. Yet without forgiveness, the sin that weighs us down will never be lifted.

The wonder of Christ is that he offers grace with such freedom that it astounds us. His offering of grace helps us come to him with our sins and seek his face. We can be confident in repentance because we know that forgiveness is certain through him. However, the other side of grace is our willingness to extend that grace to those who have sinned against us. Christ calls us to forgive others as we have been forgiven (Matthew 6:12). When Christians incorporate the pattern of recognizing sin and extending grace to each other, we will go a long way toward addressing our society's racial issues. We then take the spiritual principles on which we base our faith and bring them into our solutions for racism.

Many Christians who seriously deal with racial issues have developed concepts of corporate repentance and corporate forgiveness as a biblical response to racial tension.[25] Corporate repentance and corporate forgiveness instill a Christian understanding of sin and grace into racial issues. I will discuss those concepts in more depth in the next two chapters.

CONCLUSION

Some people believe that time heals all wounds. But there is no guarantee that time will heal our society's racial wounds. Unless we use repentance and grace to confront our racial problems, it is not certain that race relations will be better decades from now than they are today.

We find it hard to incorporate grace into our interactions with those of other races because of fear. We fear that others will not extend grace to us when we acknowledge our own failings. Our relationships are damaged by our fear of dealing honestly and openly with our sins. Time does not heal untreated wounds; rather those wounds fester and become worse.

Whites and people of color have mutual responsibilities that they must fulfill. The sin nature is universal for people of all races, but how the sin nature manifests itself is clearly different for majority group members and for people of color. Both groups must stop going down the old paths that their sins created. If either side decides not to participate in repairing the damage, we will suffer the same racial alienation we have endured in the past. In the next two chapters we will look at the unique challenges faced by whites and racial minorities in our struggle for racial harmony.

Sin Nature and
European Americans

The sins of both majority and minority group members contribute to our society's racial conflicts, but that does not mean both groups have identical roles in the solution. The mutual responsibility model recognizes that the temptations of sin for majority group members are naturally different from the temptations of sin for racial minorities.

This may be the chapter I am least equipped to write. It is tricky for me as a person of color to write about the sins of European Americans. I am mindful of Jesus' admonition to make sure I take the plank out of my own eye before I look for the speck in someone else's eye (Matthew 7:5). But regardless of my qualifications, this chapter must be written. Too often in history the responsibility for racial harmony has been placed solely on the shoulders of people of color. We will not have racial harmony until both majority and minority group members accept and carry out their unique responsibilities.

HISTORICAL AND INSTITUTIONAL RACISM

People of color and majority group members understand racism in contrasting ways. As I pointed out in the first chapter, European Americans tend to understand racism as something that an individual does to another person. People of color have a more structuralist view of racism.[1] Because of their individualist view of racism, majority group members tend to dismiss the structuralist view, which leads them to conclude that racial issues are overblown. To overcome the barrier of ignorance, we must look at how historical and institutional racism continues to affect the lives of people of color.

It is not my purpose to look at all the ways in which racism has manifested itself in American history. I will assume that the reader has a general understanding of United States history and is aware of the ways in which people of color have been oppressed in our past, such as slavery, genocide, internment centers, reservations and economic exploitation. Instead of going into a recitation of the historic sins of racism, I want to concentrate on how those sins impact our society today.

Often I hear whites say that they should not be blamed for the injustices of the past. They personally never owned slaves, killed Indians, stole land from Hispanics or put Asians in internment centers.[2] They are quite right, but their assertions miss the bigger picture. While these majority group members did not directly participate in past racial sins, they have benefited from those sins. They enjoy their present economic standing partly because their ancestors were spared from racial discrimination. That fact raises a moral question for majority group Christians. Should Christians accept wealth that was stolen, even if they did not do the stealing?

STEALING INDIAN LAND

To illustrate how the racial oppression of previous generations has benefited European Americans, we can look at the fate of Native Americans. When Europeans arrived in North America, Indians owned all the land.[3] After the colonies were established, a process began which transferred ownership of the land from the native peoples to those in the dominant culture. The process was far from equitable. It included war, murder, threats, lies and other horrendous sins.[4] Because of these sins, this land became available to non-Indians at a relatively cheap price. It was cheap because the price was not negotiated fairly. The land was usually taken at the point of a gun. Down through our history the land was passed from one person to another until it became available to today's homeowners. Anyone who owns a home in the United States today and is not an Indian has benefited from the oppression of Native Americans.[5] I do not make that statement to induce guilt, but it is a reality that we have to face.

To a lesser degree we can also argue that majority group members have benefited from the historic enslavement of African Americans, the underpaid labor of Hispanic Americans and the economic oppression of Asian Americans. The continuing benefits do not depend on overt racism or whether European Americans have personal racial animosity. Our country's racist past continues to poison our culture and our economy. People of color are generally aware of this poison. They are legitimately upset when majority group members argue that they are innocent of any historic wrongdoing, without acknowledging that they benefit from past wrongdoings.

THE EFFECTS OF WHITE FLIGHT

If racism in history was all we had to deal with, it would be enough to create enormous barriers between majority group members and racial minorities. However, racism is not limited to overt personal bias or the effects of historic events. Racism is also manifested in the way we shape our current institutions.

The ways that social structures and institutions systematically work against the interest of people of color is called *institutional racism*. Institutional racism and historic racism are not unrelated concepts. Historic racism is the primary way institutional racism forms, especially in a society that rejects overt racism. Institutional racism based on historically racist social structures is allowed to persist because it does not appear to directly discriminate against people of color. However, social structures have great power to shape the lives of minorities.

For example, in 1937 the United States government set up the Federal Housing Administration Loan Program. It was designed to help working-class people buy their own homes. The government would guarantee the loan and lower the interest rate. The program made home ownership possible for people who had no other means of buying a home.

However, policy makers had a major concern. African Americans would also be able to purchase homes at a lower rate. Cheaper home loans created the possibility of integrated residential areas, since working-class blacks could purchase homes in the same area as working-class whites. The thought of racially integrated neighborhoods was troublesome in a society which still feared interracial friendships and marriages.[6] Segregated neighborhoods were seen as necessary to insure that interracial friendships and romantic involvements did not develop. To prevent the FHA program from being used to create multiracial neighborhoods, loans were not given to blacks if they were going to use those loans to integrate a neighborhood. As a result, white working-class families were able to leave the decaying inner cities and purchase homes in the more prosperous suburbs. Since whites heavily populated the suburbs, blacks were not able to use the program to escape the economic devastation of their inner-city communities. The program helped facilitate the process sociologists call *white flight* from poor inner city neighborhoods. If you can identify white, black, Latino or Asian neighborhoods in your city, you can see the results of white flight.

White flight is important not just because it reduces the possibility of interracial interaction between whites and blacks. It is also important because many of the majority group's resources fled with them when they left the communities of color. Trips into the predominantly black underclass sections of our larger cities will testify to this fact. Most of these areas have very little industry and few major stores. There are few jobs for those who live in these areas, unless they have the money to own a car to drive into the predominantly white areas. Of course the difficulty of a young black lower-class male getting a job in a predominantly white suburb is another problem altogether. Poor whites who live in the suburbs have more access to resources than racial minorities living in poor ghettos and barrios. In this way we can see that poverty is at least partially affected by racial segregation.

Today any black who qualifies for the FHA program can purchase a house in any neighborhood that he or she can afford. But the effect of earlier racism still shows in the housing patterns we see today. Furthermore, the historic effects create contemporary expectations which maintain residential segregation. The perception of blacks living in crime-filled neighborhoods with poor schools still exists to discourage whites from living among blacks.

I live in the Dallas-Fort Worth metroplex. More people of color than whites live in the city of Dallas and in the city of Fort Worth. But they are more likely to live in poorer inner-city areas while whites live in the more affluent suburbs. Dallas and Fort Worth are not anomalies. In every large city where I have lived, minority areas of town contrast with more affluent suburbs.[7] Even if enough affluent blacks move into a predominantly white neighborhood, we know that whites will move away and perpetuate residential segregation.[8] It is not just whites' historic racism that disadvantages people of color, it is their contemporary reluctance to have neighbors of color. Racial residential segregation is as American as apple pie.

If residential segregation is only about people living with their own kind, why should Christians care about it? The problem is that the economic gap between whites and blacks can partly be attributed to residential segregation. Residential segregation has been called the "linchpin of American race relations."[9] It is the means by which the disadvantages of racial minorities remain embedded in society.

Allow me to demonstrate one way in which residential segregation works against the interests of people of color. Education is one of the most important ways in which Americans prepare themselves for economic success. The quality of schools is very important, and the degree to which schools are financed is also important. The more funds a school receives, the more resources administrators and teachers will enjoy.

Residential segregation influences school financing because most school districts rely heavily on property taxes. If the homes in a school district have a high economic value, then the schools in that district are likely to receive the money they need. If the homes are not worth a great deal of money, then the schools will struggle to find adequate resources. Because of white flight, money has fled the minority communities. Industry and social services are less likely to be located in the inner city than in the more prosperous white suburbs. Homes in inner-city neighborhoods are less likely to hold their value. In order for property taxes to adequately fund the schools, poorer homes must be assessed at a higher tax rate.[10] The higher tax rate is laid on the very people who can least afford it. The result is that schools in poorer neighborhoods fail to get the funding they need to do an adequate job of educating children.[11]

Notice that the educational funding system, not individuals themselves, discriminates against people of color. To my knowledge there is no group of whites sitting in some smoke-filled room trying to figure out how to keep people of color from going to better schools. Fifty years ago we would have seen that type of racism. Today's racial discrimination is more institutional and less individual, but the effects are equally devastating.

Are we to believe that none of the gap in academic scores between whites and nonwhites is due to the educational segregation of our children, when whites are able to send their children to better-funded schools? Is it not clear that at least part of the reason why people of color do not reach the economic level of whites is that they receive an inferior education? Institutional discrimination can be just as debilitating as personal racism and just as protective of the social status of majority group members.

There are entire books that address institutional racism in areas such as residential segregation,[12] wealth[13] and crime.[14] I have only scratched the surface of how institutional discrimination impacts the lives of people of color.

CORPORATE REPENTANCE

We can see from all the evidence that institutional racism is sin. Although it is not a sin that we link to a particular person, its detrimental effects are still sinful. In racism we see the central problem that Christ came down to earth to confront. That is the problem of sin. Sin corrupted our relationship with God, and something had to be done to restore the relationship. There was a price to be paid, and Christ paid it for us.

Whether sin is due to our own individual actions or whether it is due to social structures, we must treat sin seriously. Secular philosophies downplay the importance of sin. They have lost the opportunity to provide a complete solution to racism. If our Christian faith is going to offer us a unique answer to the problem of racism, then we have to look to that faith.

Our Christian faith says that salvation comes from a process of repentance of sin and receiving forgiveness from Christ.[15] The same pattern of repentance and forgiveness that restores us to a right relationship with God also offers ways to heal our fallen race relations. In an effort to promote such healing, some Christians have developed the controversial call of corporate repentance by majority group members.[16]

Worldly philosophy would say that rather than repenting and dwelling on the past, we should look to make ourselves better in the future. But such a philosophy underestimates sin's power to continue to poison our society. We must take proactive steps to deal with sin. One of the

most important proactive steps that Christians can take is to repent of
their sins.

Here is the controversy of corporate repentance. White Christians
logically ask, "What am I to repent of?" They will point out that they do
not share the racism of their ancestors. They will insist that race is not
an issue when they seek a friend or colleague. They will argue that they
should not be held accountable for slavery, murder and oppression of
minority peoples. Their responses are reasonable for those who see sin
as only individualistic; but sin is not limited to individualistic actions.
The Bible tells us that the Lord confronted the actions of Israelite society
(Ezra 9; Amos 2:6-16; Malachi 1:6—3:15). Both Nehemiah (Nehemiah
1:6-7) and Daniel (Daniel 9:5-6) confessed not only their own personal
sins but the sins of their ancestors. Their confessions show us that sin is
not only individualistic but corporate as well.

Corporate repentance is not about whites repenting for their own personal failings, although some may need to do that. It is about sorrow for
the historic and contemporary mistreatment of people of color. Its goal is
that European Americans will be grieved to realize that they benefit from
racism even though they are not racist themselves, and they will seek to
understand more of the plight of people of color because they want to end
the pain of racism. They will begin to understand how their racial attitudes are not so benign as they thought and may contribute to the maintenance of the racial status quo. From such new awareness, whites will
act on behalf of racial minorities.[17] Bringing reconciliation will become
more important than protecting their own racial and social position.

European Americans may see the call to corporate repentance as a minority attempt to get whites to grovel before people of color. In fact racial
minorities do commit sins which justify this concern, and in the next
chapter I will address some of those sins. However, majority group
members must understand the fears of people of color. We fear that
whites are not really interested in creating a fair society. We fear that

whites want to talk about lofty concepts to distract us from the fact that society works so well for their benefit. All the talk of colorblindness and fairness can serve to mask the fact that these whites are unwilling to do anything to deal with institutional racism. In fact, concepts of colorblind racism are becoming popular in academic circles.[18] Such concerns are central to whether we can ever have racial reconciliation.

Miroslav Volf points out that peace is not the mere absence of conflict but real communion between the former combatants.[19] We will never get such communion if we ignore the rightful concerns of those who have been abused. Instead we will get the false peace we have today. It takes only one murder, one trial, one police shooting, one immigrant caught in a crime to destroy the false peace and bring the poison of racial conflict back to the surface. People of color are rightfully concerned that majority group members are satisfied with false peace.

This is why the Christian concept of corporate repentance is so important. Christians recognize that sin must be acknowledged and confronted before we can experience true racial reconciliation. White Christians who engage in corporate repentance acknowledge and confront the lingering effects of racial sin. They may not agree with Christians of color on political issues such as affirmative action and the role of government, but they are not likely to dismiss our concerns with a platitude such as "I never owned any slaves." Instead they will have a repentant attitude which compels them to listen to our concerns. They will act on those concerns even if the action is costly. Because they recognize the corporate nature of racism, they will be eager to work with us to end institutional racism. Majority group corporate repentance is an important part of the mutual responsibility model.

My wife, Sherelyn, is a white woman who has developed an attitude of corporate repentance. The attitude has served her well as she has developed interracial friendships and has participated in racial healing. For example, we were attending a Native American festival, and she went to the food stand to get something to eat. Behind the booth was a Native American man who was a war veteran. After striking up a conversation, she told him of a time she attended a Nez Perce powwow where she saw a warrior dance in honor of the United States flag.[20] The sight brought tears to her eyes because she knows enough of Indian history to know how much damage has been done under the banner of the Stars and Stripes. Yet the Nez Perce nation and that veteran at the festival had risked their lives for the country that had mistreated them. They had not even been thanked for such service. The heart of this American Indian was clearly touched. He told her, "Well, someone has thanked us now."

I do not know if that Native American veteran was a Christian. If Sherelyn had met him in a Christian context, the two of them could have explored the spiritual dimensions of his healing and her repentance. Their exploration would have made it easier for them to work together to heal the racial barriers that remain in the body of Christ. Sherelyn did not have to agree with the man on all racial issues, but her respect for his history and service opened up a conversation that enhanced racial understanding.

Sherelyn does not stop at feeling sorry for people of color. She seeks to place herself in the company of people of color so that she can learn from them, and then she can act to meet their needs. Her concern for their issues has positive consequences. For example, when a Mexican worker was injured near our property, she did not just respond as a registered nurse to his physical needs, but she was also aware of his concerns about his immigration status. She followed up with a phone call and a visit to make sure his hospital bills would be paid by his employer, and she was ready to fight against any threat of deportation. His gratitude was such that after he was released from the hospital, he came to our home to bring her a dozen roses and to personally thank her. Her attitude and actions demonstrating corporate repentance make her a first-rate racial reconciler.[21]

Unfortunately Sherelyn tends to be the exception and not the rule. If more whites lived their lives as she does, then more people of color would know that their perspectives would be heard and respected by majority group members. They would be more willing to seek partnership with whites in relationships that can lead to reconciliation. However, most majority group members show only a passing interest in racial concerns. There is evidence that white Christians are less likely than other whites to show interest in the concerns of people of color.[22] It is no wonder that Christians of color have a difficult time trusting white believers. A critical mass of majority group Christians must begin to explore how they can develop the attitude of corporate repentance. Then it will be safe for racial minorities to express their fears. Only then will we see the large-scale dialogue among believers of different races that will make a difference for all of us who desire racial harmony.

DO WE HAVE A BRIGHT FUTURE?

In this chapter I have explored our racial history and contemporary institutional discrimination. But just as it is a mistake to ignore our past, it is a mistake to focus too much on that past. The mutual responsibility model balances concerns about past sins with the need for healing in future relationships. We must think about what sort of racial future we want in our churches and in our society so that we can move toward that future.

Many white Christians envision a colorblind future. While colorblindness is laudable in theory, it is unrealistic at this time in our country. We must seek a church where no single racial group is dominant, but where all racial groups work together to provide the church with their own unique talents and gifts. The Bible talks about the members of the church as members of the body with different skills to share with each other (1 Corinthians 12:27-30). In the same way, we must seek out how to share our unique abilities with each other as we overcome racial alienation and tension. I contend that this vision, in which we celebrate and welcome our racially based cultural differences, rather than the color-blind dream, is closer to what God wants for us.

If white Christians want to be part of the solution to our society's racial problems, they must realize that their perceptions about racial issues are not the only accurate ones. Majority group members must humbly seek to learn about racial minorities and why we feel the way we do. They have to be ruthlessly honest about how they have gained and continue to gain from the racial status quo. They have to deal with the sticky question of whether and how they may need to give back some of their unearned racial advantages. Finally, they have to face the concept of corporate repentance.

As I stated earlier, whites and nonwhites do not have identical responsibilities in the mutual responsibility model. Racial minorities have a different but just as important role to play. We have our own tasks, which are no less challenging than the duties of the majority. Any solution to racism that does not include the proactive actions of people of color is incomplete. Such a solution only encourages racial arrogance and pride on the part of racial minorities, even as it disempowers them from participating in solutions to racial problems. In the following chapter I will try to flesh out the distinct responsibilities of racial minorities.

Sin Nature and
Racial Minorities

People of color are strongly tempted to deny any responsibility for racial healing. Many believe that because of the abuse they have suffered at the hands of the majority, they are the only victims of racism.[1] It is natural for racial minorities to focus on their own sufferings rather than how they may have contributed to racial strife. But such a limited focus leaves the task of racial healing half done. People of color can and do sin against majority group members. Our wounded race relations cannot be healed unless both the majority and minorities play an active part in the healing.

Those who absolve racial minorities of all responsibility show a lack of understanding about our sin nature. Racial minorities have been and continue to be victims of racism. But even victims have a sin nature. Jesus' call for repentance covers victims as well as oppressors.[2] We do the victims no favor if we downplay the reality of their sin nature. We rob the victims of the opportunity to confront their own weaknesses. We also discourage fellowship between majority group members and racial minorities if we tell minorities that they have no responsibility to reach out to European Americans. The mutual responsibility model, unlike the multiculturalist and white responsibility models, is balanced in its approach. It compels us to look at the responsibilities of people of color as well as the tasks of majority group members.

In this chapter I will explore the way our sin nature poisons the thoughts and actions of racial minorities. First I will show how racial minorities use their status as victims to sin against majority group members. Then I will look at the importance of renewing our relationships with majority group members. Racial minorities often focus only on justice, but Christians of color must strive for a Christlike balance of justice and love. I will explore an attitude of forgiveness and will challenge racial minorities to rise above their own bias and help create mutually respectful, even loving, relationships with majority group members.

THE RACE CARD

In *Breaking Down Walls,* Glen Kehrein writes about working with a black minister who began an adulterous affair.[3] When Kehrein confronted the man about his sin, the minister accused him of racism. The minister knew that since Kehrein was a white man striving to deal with racial issues, the charge of racism would be a useful tool to deflect accusations of sin. Here is a clear example of playing the race card. Kehrein was not a racist. The charge of racism was not made in order to further the cause of racial justice. The accusation was made to help a person of color escape his legitimate responsibilities. It was the sort of dodge that should be exposed as an illegitimate claim to power.

Few actions damage race relations more than playing the race card. It is even more destructive than the racial insensitivity of white Christians because it is an intentional attempt to use one's racial status to escape responsibility and deny one's sin. When it happens, it breaks the trust between people of different races. People of color have taken the good intentions of the majority and squandered their goodwill in order to further our own selfish desires. How are European Americans going to believe our claims of racism when they see us use those claims to get away with sin, to escape our responsibilities and to punish those we do not like?

We can cite many other examples of playing the race card. Illinois congressman Mel Reynolds was caught having sex with a teenager, and he claimed to be the victim of racism. He attempted to use the accusation of racism to escape charges of statutory rape. The head of the National Basketball Players Association, Billy Hunter, played the race card when he accused NBA commissioner David Stern of racism during their negotiations, when Stern was merely engaging in hardball negotiating tactics. Students of color play the race card when they are too lazy to study and then complain that the teacher hates them because of their race. From my position in academia I have often observed students who try this.

When accusations of racism are made only to further the selfish interests of racial minorities, it becomes more difficult for people of color to point out real racism. We do not give the majority any reason to listen to us if we abuse the privilege. If we cry wolf at any imagined racist incident, then when racism really happens, few will pay attention to us.

If we fully understand the concept of human depravity, we should not be surprised that people play the race card. People of color want a social weapon they can use to obtain what they want. It seems to be in our interest to make accusations of racism that help us bully whites around. Are you not getting a good grade in class? Accuse the teacher of racism and see if you can get your grade up a notch. Have you been caught doing seventy-five in a fifty-five-mile-per-hour zone? Say that the cop had it in for you because of your race, and maybe you can get a warning instead of a ticket. Are you not being promoted fast enough for your liking? Threaten to file a civil rights lawsuit, then prepare to move into that corner office.

The sad truth is that racism may very well be part of all those situations. Teachers still have low expectations of minorities' academic work. Racial profiling is a documented fact in the United States.[4] Companies do not always promote people of color as readily as they deserve.[5] Racism is more subtle than in the past, and we should make a careful analysis of each of these situations to assess whether racism is a factor. Blind accusations of racism only hinder an accurate picture of what is going on. When we truly find racism and tell our white friends, they will not believe us. We will lose them as potential allies. We will pay for the grade, the warning or the promotion with an inability to deal with the larger racial issues that plague our society.

Sometimes racism is overt and clear to the victims. In those cases the victims are obligated to bring it to the attention of the proper authorities and/or confront the perpetrator of racism. Sometimes racism is subtle and less clear to the victims. In those cases the victims are obligated to discuss the situation with the person who may be engaging in racism so the person has a chance to learn and grow. Sometimes it is unclear whether racism is to blame. In those cases the possible victims should bring the situation to the attention of the possible perpetrators in a non-accusatory manner in order to discover the truth. If people of color handle apparent racism in such a way, we will be able to promote racial healing. If we handle every situation with a demanding racial accusation, then majority group members will not want to work with us. The majority will see racial problems not as a moral issue but as a power struggle. Whites will seek to cover up their wrongs if they are guilty and will strike back at us if they are innocent.

Whites are not the source of this racial sin, and they are not the solution. Playing the race card is our problem, not the problem of majority group members. If you are a person of color, it is not enough that you do not personally play the race card. Whites are generally defenseless against unfounded accusations of racism. Christians of color must fight against unjust accusations. If a situation looks suspicious, we must say so.

For example, in Kehrein's situation with the adulterous minister, consider the potential effect of black Christians telling the black minister to stop cheating on his wife. If Christians of color had rallied around Kehrein and said they would not allow the black minister to deny his sin, then the minister would have had to confront his own shortcomings. He would have had a chance to grow in an accountability relationship with Kehrein. Instead the black minister split the ministry along racial lines and badly damaged the trust that Kehrein had won. Kehrein became gun-shy about working in a multiracial setting until a black minister with more integrity, the coauthor of his book, came into his life.

We people of color have the ability to stop unfair accusations of racism, but we often choose not to because we want to get back at whites. We only hurt ourselves in the long run. We see it all the time. A black community leader makes racial accusations that have no basis. We know the charges are unfounded, but we support the leader anyway because we do not want to be traitors to the cause. As a Christian I would rather betray some racial cause than betray the truth that has set me free.

Playing the race card has no place in the mutual responsibility model. Christians of color should be the first ones to confront anyone who is obviously playing this card. As a Christian I should seek out my white brothers and sisters because I want what is best for them. It is best for them if I inform them about racism that they may not see. I will not make unsubstantiated accusations of racism. Such accusations only serve to further my selfish desires.

It is right for people of color to want equal power, respect and authority with our white brothers and sisters. But I fear that many of us want more than equality. Many of us want a superior position over European Americans, and playing the race card is a way to incrementally obtain that goal. Over time, if we play the race card enough, we can get whites to acquiesce to our demands. We can even convince ourselves that this is fair, given our society's history of racial abuse. The practice quickly becomes a way to abuse our white brothers and sisters. We racial minorities must recognize playing the race card as sin and be prepared to confess it when it happens.

ARE REPARATIONS THE ANSWER?

In recent years we have heard the call for reparations for racial minorities, especially for African Americans. Proposed reparations take various forms, but advocates of the white responsibility and multiculturalism models argue that society owes people of color some type of payment for historic and contemporary oppression.

Some mistakenly believe that reparations mean a check will be sent out to every individual African American. In fact, those who support reparations argue that reparations should be paid to the group rather than to the individual.[6] Payment should come from the United States government or from large businesses. The money is not to come from individual whites. The funds would be given to organizations that would decide how to spend it to further the economic, educational and political aspirations of African Americans.

The justification for group repayment is that the horrors of slavery and racism were done to African Americans as a group, and the group should be repaid for the harm they have suffered. Reparations are seen as the payment of a bill which the United States government and certain businesses owe blacks. They are not based on whether or not blacks need the money.[7]

Payment of reparations would not be limited to blacks in the United States. Supporters of reparations hold that racism is an international crime by which the United States and European nations colonized nations of color. Therefore nations of color should receive reparations as well.[8]

Reparations are generally seen as a starting point and not as a final settlement. Those who call for reparations contend that the debt owed to African Americans can never be paid by money alone. Reparations are the righteous repayment for the labor, property and other economic resources the dominant group seized from African Americans throughout the centuries. Only after reparations have been paid can we create true civil equality.[9]

If it has done nothing else, talk of reparations has produced a useful racial dialogue.[10] The discussion has provided a forum to explore ways in which European Americans have benefited from racism. To the degree that the issue of reparations has allowed us to gain a more complete understanding of the horrors of racism and how it is still a part of our society, the discussion has been valuable.

However, there is a dark side to reparations. What would happen if our government did pay? It would take an enormous amount of money.[11] Any European American who pays taxes would be paying for reparations. How would whites react to that? While advocates claim it would help mend damaged racial relationships, I think most whites would see it as nothing but a big payoff. They would not want to hear any more about racism or racial difficulties. Discussion about racial issues would become impossible. A majority group member who heard further complaints about racism would say, "They've been paid off. Why are they whining now? They just want more money from us."

Reparations would guarantee that healing relationships between whites and people of color would not take place. The communion that Volf discusses[12] and the *shalom* that Plantinga envisions[13] would be traded for economic gain. I would oppose the payment of official reparations by our government unless it can be done in a way that promotes rather than represses the possibility of positive race relations. While I think that the discussion produced by the idea of reparations is excellent, I do not include the actual payment of reparations as part of the mutual responsibility model.

WHAT ABOUT JUSTICE?

Reparations represent one extreme of the dimensions of racial power. The opposite extreme is to focus on relationships and ignore the disproportionate power of whites in our society. That would be a serious mistake. To forget about racial justice means that we can never confront the racial sickness in our society. While reparations would eliminate the possibility of developing healthy race relations, we will still not develop those relationships if we sacrifice our desire for justice.

In fact we do not have to sacrifice justice for healthy relationships. We can gain justice through healthy relationships. By developing relationships with European Americans, we can enlist them as allies in our quest for racial justice. My personal experience as a teacher of race relations in college and my interpersonal relations indicate that we do not have to capitulate on justice to gain the friendship of our white brothers and sisters. As long as we do not abuse the race card, and they see that we are trying to expose genuine racism, we will be able to show them the need for racial justice. The mutual responsibility model is not a call to ignore racial justice; it is a way to promote justice through loving interracial relationships.

I once heard a speaker say that the aim of psychotherapy is to create an atmosphere in which people can look at their shortcomings. Then the therapist can confront the client with issues that need to be addressed. However, the therapist will not create such an atmosphere if the client only thinks that the therapist wants to accuse him or her of being wrong. The therapist has to earn the right to be heard by the client.

In the same way, we people of color need to create an environment in which whites can learn about the reality of racism. But we have to earn the right to be heard, or whites will believe we are only trying to rip them off. We must confront our majority group brothers and sisters in ways that show that we truly care about them, even as we grieve for the racism that victimizes us. We will be right in what we say but wrong in how we say it if we fail to say it with love and respect. We will enlist many more of the majority in our struggle for racial justice if we speak in the context of sincere friendship rather than condemnation.

CORPORATE FORGIVENESS

Only after we understand the tension between justice and relationship can we tackle the controversial concept of corporate forgiveness. In chapter seven I discussed how Christianity leads the way to dealing with sin through corporate repentance. The attitude of corporate repentance is necessary among majority group Christians in order to assure racial minorities that whites will be there to help them in their struggles.

The other side of the coin is corporate forgiveness. Racial minorities have responsibilities in this tremendous task of racial reconciliation. Just as we need assurance that whites will not neglect our legitimate concerns, majority group members also need assurance that their expressions of repentance and white guilt will not be used against them. A scripturally accurate attitude of corporate forgiveness can give majority group members such assurance. Just as corporate repentance is an essential part of the mutual responsibility model, so is corporate forgiveness.

Sometimes after I have an argument with a friend, the friend comes back and asks for forgiveness. Sometimes I say that I forgive him or her, but in the back of my mind I think, *Yeah, the next time I want something from that person, I have an ace to play.* I have not really forgiven the person. Saying "I forgive you" is canny strategy at that point of the relationship. That is how we minority Christians sometimes treat repentance. We try to sound very spiritual by telling whites that they are forgiven, but at the first opportunity we use white guilt to get what we want. As a result, whites learn not to trust us.

If white Christians approach us with an attitude of corporate repentance, we must reciprocate with an attitude of corporate forgiveness. This does not mean we must keep silent about racial injustice. If white Christians have approached us with a real attitude of corporate repentance, they will be even more open to remedying injustice. But we must recognize that by forgiving them we abdicate our right to bash them over the head with their own repentance. Instead we now have a responsibility to work with them and listen to their concerns.

It sounds easier to forgive than to repent until you realize that when you forgive, you give up the right to have an ace to play later. Other people have hurt us, and we want to be paid back for the pain we have suffered. Christian forgiveness is not only difficult; it can even feel unfair. We will do well to remember the many times Jesus has forgiven us when we did not deserve it. Forgiveness is the core of our faith. By forgiving those who have harmed us, we can help them grow as reconcilers in ways that are not possible if they are always under the accusation of racism.

If ever anyone had a right to withhold forgiveness, it would be Desmond Tutu. Having personally experienced the horror of South African apartheid, by human standards Tutu had every right to hold bitterness and anger toward whites. Instead he realized that such an attitude would only feed the alienation of apartheid. He beautifully tells of the development of the Truth and Reconciliation Commission and his path toward forgiveness in his book *No Future Without Forgiveness*.[14] Tutu discusses the power of an apology from the white South Africans, but more importantly he focuses on why he embarked on a path to forgiveness. Tutu points out that when people who have been abused gain power, they tend to abuse those who were their oppressors. They do not realize that their former oppressors may one day regain power and the cycle of abuse will continue. The only way to break the cycle of abuse is to be ready to forgive one's former oppressors.

I believe that if blacks ever gain as much power over whites as whites have had over blacks, we will see blacks set up rules which allow them to exploit whites. If given the opportunity, blacks would even enslave the majority group.[15] I believe that if Indians had the opportunity to exploit and murder whites, they would do so.[16] I believe that Asian and Hispanic Americans would oppress European Americans if they got the chance. Throughout our history, whites have sinned against people of color more than people of color have sinned against whites. Whites sin not because they are white but because they are human. Events in places such as Sudan, Rwanda and Afghanistan show that sin is not limited to Europeans and European Americans. We people of color have no right to feel arrogance and pride over majority group members because we have not perpetuated racial abuse to the same degree as whites. Our task is to learn to forgive, or we will forever be trapped in a cycle of oppression and revenge.

Am I asking a lot from those who have been abused? Yes, I am. Tutu observes that reconciliation is not cheap. He points out that it cost God his own Son. Forgiveness means that we give up the right to pay back our former oppressors with the same injustice they showed us. Forgiveness allows us the opportunity to break the awful cycle of hate and revenge.

There are people of color who will read these words and argue that the pain is too great. They may feel that they cannot trust whites unless they keep the race card handy. They believe that forgiveness is too easy on majority group members, and they are entitled to hold on to their resentment. I respect their fears and concerns. But if we are to seek healthy and egalitarian relationships with majority group members, where power can be equally shared, then we have to give up the right to attack them with our demands whenever we feel insecure. Instead, we must go through the difficult process of forgiving, just as our ultimate role model, Jesus Christ, taught us. We must believe that he will provide us with the resources we need to enter into that state of forgiveness. Finally, we must trust our white brothers and sisters to take our concerns seriously and to work with us so we can understand and support each other out of love instead of guilt.

MINORITIES RELATING TO EACH OTHER

An examination of the responsibilities of people of color is incomplete unless it includes a look at the relationship of people of color to each other. When we speak of corporate repentance, we are talking about what whites should do for people of color. Institutional, systematic racism is something that whites have done to people of color and not the other way around. However, people of color must consider corporate repentance for the sins they have committed against other people of color. The use of buffalo soldiers to hunt down Native Americans is an example. African Americans would do well to think about how they can help Native Americans, given the role of African Americans in Native disenfranchisement.[17]

Racial minorities do sin against each other, and there is a need for healing between them. For example, we cannot ignore the arrogance of some Asian Americans toward African Americans and the corresponding violence done to Asian Americans by African Americans. We can argue that whites created the society that sets up this sort of conflict, but we cannot absolve minorities of their own guilt. Racial minorities need to reconnect with other people of color if we want to experience complete racial healing.

There is another important reason why minority Christians should work to resolve hostility with other Christians of color. If we do so, we will gain legitimacy in the eyes of majority group members. Resolution of conflict among people of color can demonstrate how we want to be treated by whites. If I as an African American am willing to work for more just immigration laws, even though the issue does not directly affect my community, then I am more able to ask for changes in laws that adversely affect my community. It is hard for people of color to ask whites to consider the interests of our racial group if we do not consider the interests of other racial groups.

MOVING TO NEW EGALITARIAN RELATIONSHIPS

For hundreds of years in our country we have suffered from oppressive hierarchical race relations. A few decades of civil rights legislation has not removed this sinful stain from our society. Racial strife will not disappear simply because we wish that everything were harmonious. Even paying off people of color cannot produce the healing balm for racial wounds. No, we must do the hard work of tearing down barriers placed in the way of new egalitarian racial relationships. I hope it does not take hundreds of years to tear down these barriers.

I believe that the mutual responsibility model offers us the promise of accelerating racial healing if we obey the call of God on our lives. Only if both whites and nonwhites take their responsibilities seriously can we overcome the effects of centuries of racial alienation. A damaged relationship can be restored only when both parties are willing to work at the healing process. We need each other if we are going to show the non-Christian world what a Christian solution to racism looks like. We must work together as Christians, not against each other as members of different racial groups, if we are to fulfill the promise of the mutual responsibility model.

It is my prayer that I have been able to provide an honest assessment which is useful for anyone, whether a majority group member or a racial minority, who is willing to take the hard steps toward racial reconciliation. The mutual responsibility model demands that we all focus on our own role in racial healing rather than how to place the blame on people of another race. My hope is that the challenges I have thrown out to both majority and minority group members will stifle the pride of different racial groups and help us see that all of us must work together to achieve true racial healing, first in the body of Christ and then in the larger society.

Jesus: The Ultimate Reconciler

If the mutual responsibility model is based on our Christian faith, then we should be able to see elements of it in the life of Jesus. As a Christian I have been taught that Jesus lived a perfect life.[1] Jesus also had to deal with those who differed from him ethnically.[2] There is scriptural support for the idea that Jesus initially came to reach the Jewish people but soon extended his ministry to non-Jews.[3] His outreach to non-Jews allows us to see how he approaches intergroup relations.

We are in an especially good situation to learn from Jesus' life because he was neither at the top nor the bottom of his society. At times he was a member of the majority group and at times he was part of the minority group. As a Jew he was an ethnic minority in a society dominated by the Romans. However, other groups had less social status than the Jews. Furthermore, Jesus was a Jewish teacher and therefore had higher status than many other Jews in his society. We can see how Jesus reacted to situations in which he had a superior social position and situations in which he had an inferior social position.

The first area we should examine is the value Jesus placed on reconciliation. Some may ask whether reconciliation is important. The Bible talks about reconciling humans to God, but why is it so important that humans be reconciled to each other? I will address that issue before I

look at how Jesus interacted with those of a lower social status than himself and then with those in a higher social position. Finally I will look at
the life of Jesus as the ultimate balance between the need to use power
wisely and the need for relationships.

Jesus Prays for Us

Mark DeYmaz, a pastor friend of mine, recently blessed me with a valuable teaching about the importance of oneness in the Christian body.
The teaching comes from John 17. It was the night of Jesus' impending
arrest. Jesus knew that he was going to die for us in only a few hours.
Jesus prayed first for his disciples and then for the rest of us (John
17:20). While everything that Jesus said is of great importance, these
words must be especially valuable since they are among the last lessons
of his mortal life.

Jesus prayed to his Father for unity among believers, that we would
all be one "so that the world may believe that you have sent me" (John
17:21). If Christians are unified, then the world will believe that God
sent Jesus. The two actions are connected. The evidence that Jesus was
sent by God is the fact that those who call on his name are one. We often
go to Jesus to ask things from him in prayer. But reconciling ourselves to
each other is actually a way we can answer Jesus' own prayer. It becomes
clear that doing the work of racial reconciliation is doing the work of
Jesus. Reconciliation is not some side issue that we can engage in if we
want. If we are going to be an answer to Jesus' prayer, then we have to
find ways to unify alienated believers.

The opposite of Jesus' prayer can happen as well. If Christians do not
become one, the world will fail to know that Jesus has been sent by the
Father. When we have segregated churches and when Christians perpetuate racial misunderstandings, then it becomes easier for non-Christians
to argue that there is no special power among Christians. We argue, fight
and bicker like everyone else. We are less powerful witnesses because we

fail to become reconciled, first within the body of Christ and second in the larger society, which suffers from the pain of racial division.

If Jesus took reconciliation so seriously, then we would expect him to model reconciliation in his own life. Jesus' middle position in the society of his day allowed him to demonstrate how to deal with intergroup hostility. First we will look at how Jesus acted when he had a superior social position. In Roman society there were groups who were lower than the Jews. Although the Romans held political control, they allowed Jews to run their own local affairs. The prejudices of the Jews often showed in the way they handled local issues. The Samaritans were the targets of Jewish prejudice. How Jesus dealt with Samaritans shows us how Christians should act when we are part of the majority group.

JESUS AND THE WOMAN AT THE WELL

In 2 Kings 17 we learn that Israel was exiled to Assyria. The king of Assyria replaced the Israelites who had lived in Samaria with people from Babylon, Cuthah, Avva, Hamath and Sepharvaim (2 Kings 17:24). These people did not worship the Lord, and he punished them with wild animals. So the king of Assyria sent some of the Israelites back to that area to teach the people about the Lord. The migration set up a situation in which many Jews would intermarry with foreigners. The people who arose from this intermixing were eventually called the Samaritans. The Jews came to look down on the Samaritans as half-breed foreigners who had been forced on the Jews. It is not surprising that the Jews resented the Samaritans and treated them as a despised minority group.

The Jews did not even respect the Samaritans enough to travel through their cities when they moved about. The Samaritans lived in the barrio or ghetto of their day. When Jesus "had to go through Samaria" on his way from Judea to Galilee (John 4:4), he was making a political statement. He was saying that we cannot pretend that our intergroup differences are illusions. We must meet these differences with intentional actions. Jesus recognized the incompleteness of a colorblindness approach to hostile relationships.

In Samaria Jesus sat down by Jacob's well while the disciples went to find food. The Samaritan woman who arrived at the well could not have been at a lower position in the social order. She was a minority. She was a woman. Because she had to come to get water in the middle of the day, we know that she was not rich. Jesus clearly enjoyed a higher social position. So how did he approach her? Did he begin to teach her and help her? No. He asked her for help. He asked her for a drink of water (John 4:7). The member of the majority group made himself vulnerable to the member of the minority. His approach was exactly opposite what we would expect from the Anglo-conformity model. Jesus' actions show that people from all walks of life have something to offer. Jesus did not come into the encounter with an attitude of arrogance and paternalism but in weakness and need.

The Samaritan woman was amazed that Jesus would request anything from her because that was simply not the way things were done in Samaria. If a Jewish male did come through Samaria, he certainly would not waste his time talking to a Samarian woman. Because Jesus treated her as a person instead of as a ministry project, she opened up to him. He began to talk to her of living water. The woman had trouble understanding the spiritual nature of the conversation, but she knew that she was tired of coming to the well. So she asked for this living water. Jesus wanted her to understand the full consequences of accepting this water. She had to deal with the sins in her life. He made a request that would show her how sin had wrecked her life. He asked her to go get her husband, knowing that she had been married five times and was now living with a man without the covering of marriage (John 4:16-18). Jesus, as a member of the majority, called a member of the minority to account for her sins. Even though he treated her with respect, he would not let her believe that all her problems came from her lower social status. Her actions had led her to develop an unseemly reputation and made her life harder. Her own sin nature had led to decisions that placed her in an even more difficult position.

Jesus' approach is contrary to what we would expect from a white responsibility model. That model would correctly identify that the woman was a victim of societal forces, and it would place nearly the entire responsibility for her problems on those social forces. But such an approach would fail to give the woman what she needed for a complete life. She needed to come to grips with how her own sin nature had contributed to her social situation. Blaming the majority group for her position in life would be inaccurate and ultimately disempowering. By being held accountable for her own actions, she could begin to take the steps to eternal life, and no one in the majority could prevent her from taking those steps.

The woman reacted in the way most of us react when we are confronted with our sins. She tried to change the subject. She began to talk about where the Samaritans worshiped (John 4:19-20). She attempted to assert the rightness of her culture over Jewish culture. For Jesus the argument was not important. It does not matter so much where we worship but what we worship. He said that the Samaritans did not know what they were worshiping (John 4:22). Jesus did not bother to critique their culture in other areas, but he held his ground concerning who should be worshiped. Advocates of the multiculturalist model are correct when they hesitate to critique other cultures on unimportant issues. But on the important issue of what worship is, Jesus did not practice a multiculturalist approach. He enunciated a path that was not relativistic. Jesus demonstrated that there will be times when one group must correct the cultural errors of another group.

The rest of John 4 relates the results of Jesus' encounter with the Samaritan woman. She not only accepted his living water; she eagerly told others about the Christ (John 4:28-30). Many Samaritans were reached because of Jesus' ministry to this woman who was one of the lowest members of her community. The way in which we minister to those of different racial or ethnic groups has long-range consequences. If we minister in a wrong manner, then we fail to have a real impact on minority communities.

None of the models from part one of this book could have provided a sufficient framework for Jesus to minister to the Samaritan woman. First he had to establish a relationship with her and show that he cared for her by making himself vulnerable to her. He did not ignore her lower social position but went out of his way to meet her at the well. He did not come in with a paternalistic attitude but showed her that he was willing to receive from her. However, he did make demands on the Samaritan woman. She had to adjust her spiritual and even her cultural thinking so she could receive all Jesus had for her. She had to deal with her own sins as well as the structural oppression of her society.

Jesus mixed the strengths of the four secular models in a way that removed their weaknesses. He created a relationship in which there was mutual responsibility between him and the woman. Jesus provided us with a template of mutual responsibility, which allowed him to bring healing into the life of this woman and the Samaritan community.

The disciples also benefited from Jesus' encounter with the woman at the well. They were not too crazy about going through Samaria themselves. I can imagine them thinking, *Doesn't Jesus know that we should avoid this neighborhood?* They were creatures of their culture. Like the woman, they were more concerned about physical food than spiritual nourishment (John 4:31-33). But Jesus took the opportunity to teach them that the message of the gospel must be taken to non-Jewish society. They could not keep it to themselves. I cannot help but think that these lessons became more meaningful after Jesus' death, when the disciples started their intercultural spreading of the gospel.

JESUS AND THE ROMANS

Jesus was not always part of the majority group. He lived in an area where the Jews were forced to accept Roman rule. The typical Roman saw Jesus as part of a conquered race. How Jesus interacted with the Romans gives us insight into principles that can be incorporated into a Christian mutual responsibility model. Because of Jesus' unique mission to come and die for us, I will not look at the last days of his life and his interaction with the Roman governor Pilate. I believe those interactions were unique to his mission and it is unwise to generalize from them.

The best accounts of Jesus dealing with the Romans are found in the Gospel of Matthew. Matthew had been a tax collector, a collaborator with the Romans. He had more intimate knowledge of the Roman rulers than the other Gospel writers. Matthew made money off the oppressive system of the Romans. He could rightly be seen as a sellout. When Jesus called him to be a disciple, Jesus risked being linked to the Roman occupiers.[4] Yet Jesus did not hesitate to reach out to Matthew. Even though Jesus' twelve disciples were Jews, Matthew's political philosophy and cultural awareness were driven more by his allegiance to Rome than by his Jewish upbringing. Imagine how the other disciples must have felt taking on this collaborator. From the very beginning Jesus was signaling that we must overcome our prejudices toward others if we are going to be a part of his movement. He required the conquered Jews to take in one of the despised Jewish traitors and treat him as a brother. As we deal with those who have done us wrong, we must remember that they may one day be our brothers and sisters in the Lord.

In Matthew's account we also read about Jesus' encounter with the Roman centurion (Matthew 8:5-13). The centurion came on behalf of his servant, and he displayed great faith in Christ. The oppressor came to the oppressed to ask for a favor. Jesus could have brought Jewish grievances to the centurion's attention. But he did not do that. Instead he concentrated on the faith it would take for a powerful centurion to humble himself and come to a Jew for help. Have you ever noticed how difficult it is for some people of color to recognize the good deeds of any whites? Jesus did not put such limitations on his compassion. It is not that he was unconcerned about justice. But he chose to meet this man at the point of his need rather than push for his own political agenda.

I do not know what happened to the Roman centurion after this encounter. Do you think it is possible that this man became more sympathetic to Jews? Do you think he may have become more lenient toward any Jews he had to arrest in the future? Do you think it is possible that he became an advocate for the Jews within Roman society? I do not know if those things happened, but I am confident that they were more likely to happen because Jesus met his need rather than use the situation to make demands on the Romans. Even majority group members have needs that minorities can choose to meet or not. If we choose to meet their needs, we can open up doors of possible reconciliation.

Jesus had another opportunity to push for a political agenda. The Pharisees sought to trap him with a question about paying taxes to Caesar (Matthew 22:15-22). They saw two possible responses from Jesus. One, Jesus could state that his kingdom was not of this world and his followers should give mindless obedience to the oppressive Roman government. Two, Jesus could state that the Roman government was too cruel to deserve allegiance and Jews should protest by withholding their taxes. Either response would be fine with the Pharisees. The first would alienate Jesus from his own oppressed people; the second would allow them to brand Jesus as a political rebel, and they could enlist the Romans in their effort to destroy him.

Jesus did not give either of the two expected answers. He said to give the government its due and to give God his due. He did not affirm the Roman government, but neither did he put priority on overthrowing the government. Jesus did not express complacency with the Roman government, but he warned against measuring the success of our Christian faith by our political success. His answer indicates that the core of the gospel is neither surrendering to corrupt political forces nor waging a political struggle against those forces.

Then was Jesus unconcerned about societal evil? Such a conclusion is not compatible with an honest reading of the Gospels. While the society of that time did not share our concept of racial differences, the Bible records many times in which Jesus sought to address the structural sins of his day. It was Jesus who talked about hungering and thirsting after righteousness (Matthew 5:6). It was Jesus who condemned the Pharisees who tithed mint but neglected justice (Luke 11:42). It was Jesus who challenged the haves in his society to give to the have-nots so they can completely follow him (Mark 10:17-31). It was Jesus who taught that God will see that justice is given to those who cry out to him (Luke 18:7-8). Finally, it was Jesus who told us that God will take away gains obtained by illegitimate methods and give them to those who are more deserving (Matthew 21:33-44).

Let us not mistake Jesus' unwillingness to participate in the political struggle against the Romans for a disinterest in justice. But notice that Jesus chose to address the structural sins of his own people more than that of the Romans. He was hardly unaware of Roman oppression, but he focused on getting the Jewish house in order first. We are to address our own sins before we focus on the sins of others.

We people of color are sometimes more willing to address the sins of majority group members than we are to address the sins within our own community. So much of the way we articulate issues of racial reconciliation is tied to our political goals that we begin to hate those who disagree with us. Instead of promoting racial reconciliation, we create more racial hostility if we use a political litmus test to determine whom we can befriend. People of color need to follow Jesus' example and refuse to prioritize political alliances over spiritual concerns.

But we also have to recognize that Jesus' actions mean that majority group members must think about issues of racial justice. European Americans still enjoy the highest racial position in our society. As I noted before, Jesus constantly challenged those with higher social positions to provide justice for those in lower social positions. Since pursuing justice was a critical part of Jesus' ministry, I have little doubt that if he were a white in the United States today, he would pursue racial justice as well. Addressing issues of racial justice must be an integral part of the mutual responsibility model, and if majority group members want to be an advocate of that model, they need to become open to learning about white privilege and institutional racism as well as willing to eradicate these social inequities.

JESUS: THE PERFECT EXAMPLE OF POWER AND RELATIONSHIP

In Jesus we see the balance that we rarely see in our society. We see a man who, whether he was part of the majority or minority, sought relationships but also addressed issues of power. It is tempting for us racial minorities to choose power rather than pursue relationships with the majority. After all, we can justify our stance by arguing that whites have dominated us for so long that it is right for us to dominate for a change. That is a human way of looking at race relations, but it is not in keeping with the mutual responsibility model. Furthermore, it is easy for majority group members to talk about just relationships without being willing to address the issues of power in a racialized society. It is in the interest of the majority to maintain their advantages and to concentrate on the warm feelings drummed up in interracial Christian circles. Relationships and warm feelings are important, but they are insufficient if we do not also address the structural racial sins of society.

The only way to completely deal with racial sins is to stop being satisfied with incomplete solutions that focus either on relationships or on confrontation. Instead, Christians should look to Christ as our ultimate role model. A careful reading of the Gospels shows that even as he sought relationships with members of other ethnic groups, Jesus also dealt with issues of oppression and justice. He reached down to a woman who was considered inferior to him, and he did so on her terms rather than his own. He served Romans without playing guilt games with them. He refused to let his kingdom become entangled with the Roman kingdom on the issue of taxes. Jesus' actions do not conform to any of the four secular models. Rather, they fit a model in which we have mutual responsibility to each other.

Finally, it is noteworthy that in all of his encounters with people of different groups, Jesus never deviated from the truth. He was truthful to the woman at the well about her sin. He honestly praised the centurion's faith. He was honest about the Roman government's right to levy taxes. Often we distort or exaggerate the truth in order to gain something for ourselves or for our racial group. Jesus refused to do this. Only when we engage in truthful dialogue can we develop the intergroup relationships that bring healing to race relations. Such truth will also bring with it the need to address unjust power differences. Honesty will produce the proper balance of relationships and power in interracial interactions.

CONCLUSION

Jesus provided different lessons for those in the majority and those in the minority. To those in the majority Jesus showed that it is inappropriate to focus on the maintenance of their own social position. He also indicated that it is appropriate to address sin among racial minorities, but never in a spirit of superiority. It is in the spirit of coming to people of color as equals, willing to be vulnerable to them, that majority group members can develop relationships that lead to racial reconciliation. Finally, if we take Jesus' actions toward structural sins seriously, then majority group Christians must be willing to get their own house in order before they attempt to address the problems of communities of color.

To people of color Jesus showed that even though he had concerns about societal evil, political revolution was not the heart of his ministry. His call for justice could be heard more clearly because he showed his love and care for those who differed from him. The life of Jesus challenges racial minorities to seek out and serve those who are not of their race, even as we pursue racial justice. If those of us who are racial minorities want to play an important role in racial healing, we have to imitate Jesus' ability to mix loving intergroup relationships with the call for social justice.

Often what stops us from fulfilling our duties to each other is the fear that the other group will misuse our good intentions. People of color fear that majority group members will not take their concerns seriously, while whites worry that racial minorities will use tactics such as the race card to take advantage of them. Fear is such a feature of our racial failures that it deserves special attention. In the next chapter I will look at the role of fear in maintaining racial hostility and mistrust.

The Fear Factor

Fear is a powerful emotion. Fear can paralyze us from taking any action or it can motivate us to take desperate measures. Fear may be rational, such as the reasonable fear of a soldier being sent to war. It can be illogical, such as the fear of a paranoid person who refuses to leave the house. Fear can motivate us to help others so that we can win their favor, or it can convince us that other people are enemies we must destroy. Much of what we do, we do in response to our fears.

In 2 Timothy 1:7 we are told that God has not given us a spirit of fear but of power, love and self-discipline. Paul positions fear as the opposite of love. Fear can stymie love and limit the power of love to create intimacy. If racial groups are to overcome our historic mistrust and learn to embrace each other, we have to overcome our fears.

Fear is a product of our sin nature. It interferes with our relationships with others through a variety of mechanisms. We may lash out at others so we hurt them before they hurt us.[1] We may hide our feelings and thoughts from others so they cannot use them as weapons against us.

Fear is a powerful factor in race relations today. The mere accusation of racism can create fear since nobody wants to be called a racist. People fear that others will not take them seriously, a common fear among people of color. Fear prevents people of different races from being honest with each other and from hearing what other people say.

I believe that our faith can help us overcome racial barriers by helping us eliminate our fears. God did not give us these fears, but he will give us the strength to overcome them.

LOVE AND FEAR IN THE CLASSROOM

In my classroom I distinctly see the fear created by dysfunctional race relations. It is a tradition that people do not talk about race, politics or religion in polite company. Yet I teach race/ethnicity courses in which I want my students to engage with me and with each other on a wide variety of racial issues. I see that people of color are afraid that their concerns will be minimized or laughed at. I sense that whites are apprehensive about expressing their concerns because of potential accusations of racism. In a classroom setting where I want to encourage honest conversation, I can clearly see the stifling effects of fear.

For me this fear means that I must be very careful when I encounter my white students. Because I am an African American, whites may be fearful of me. I worry less about the willingness of my students of color to raise racial concerns because I know that I will be bringing up the issues myself. But to be a child of God means that I have to die to my sins (Romans 6:11). One of my biggest sins is feeding my own selfish desires. Part of dying to my selfishness is learning to see things from other people's perspectives. I cannot allow myself the luxury of finding excuses to ignore the concerns of my white students and friends. Rather I must put aside my own concerns so that I can serve others.

I must learn to put aside fear by expressing love. When I go out of my way to allow white students to express their frustrations, that is an expression of love that can conquer fear. At times I have admonished a student of color who made an unfair charge of racism toward a white student. If I fail to handle such a situation properly, my white students' fears will grow, and honest conversation will become impossible. My challenge is to keep the lines of dialogue open, and I believe that will happen only if I stay sensitive to the needs of my white students.

Let me be clear about one aspect of this process. It is not that I ignore the needs of students of color. Anyone who has taken a race/ethnicity class from me knows that I spend a great deal of time discussing issues of white privilege, institutional discrimination, historic racism and other issues that concern of people of color. My class is not based on the models of colorblindness, Anglo-conformity or any other philosophy that supports majority group interest over the interest of people of color. I base my teaching on the mutual responsibility model, which values the perspectives of all races. It is natural for me to organize my courses so the interests of African Americans will be expressed. That I can do without any effort. What does take effort is for me to also look out for the interests of those who are not like me—European Americans. White Christians who want to deal with fear must die to themselves and look to the interests of people of color more than their own racial interests.

DIFFERENT FEARS, DIFFERENT RESPONSIBILITIES

Majority and minority group members have distinct responsibilities in the battle against racism. These responsibilities generate different concerns for whites and nonwhites. All of us must die to ourselves, but the fears of whites are different from the fears of nonwhites. When we fail to recognize these differences, we make inaccurate attributions, which can lead to more racial confusion.

Whites are very afraid of being labeled racist. One of the worst things you can call a majority group member is a racist. The accusation raises the stereotype of a culturally bankrupt bigot. Fear prevents European Americans from being willing to enter into genuine dialogue with people of color, because they do not want to say something that will get them categorized as racist. As a result, whites avoid addressing racial issues by favoring a colorblind or Anglo-conformity perspective. If they can dismiss all discussions about race, they can relieve themselves of their fears.

People of color have fears as well. They fear that they will be ridiculed when they bring up their racial concerns. They want to see racial abuse end, and they know that it will end only if majority group members are willing to help them change society. If whites do not take their concerns seriously, their efforts will be in vain. They fear being characterized as troublemakers. They can become so determined to have racial issues taken seriously that they support anyone who points out racism. Their determination leads them to embrace the multiculturalist model or the white responsibility model.

Eventually we develop a cycle of fear that inhibits racial healing. The fears of whites lead them to ignore racial issues. Their effort to dismiss racial issues feeds the fear of people of color that racism will not be taken seriously. The fears of people of color deepen through the misguided efforts of majority group members. As a result, people of color begin to support leaders who foolishly play the race card but who at least uphold the importance of racial justice. Playing the race card and other actions of minority leaders increase the fears of whites that they will be labeled racist regardless of what they say or do. As whites' fears deepen, they redouble their efforts to push for the colorblind philosophy. The vicious circle of dysfunctional race relations continues, with the fears of whites and the fears of people of color feeding on each other.

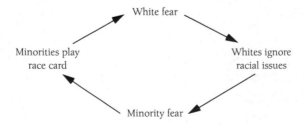

Figure 1. Vicious circle of dysfunctional race relations

None of the secular models adequately deals with our fears. That is why it is so important for Christians to develop a mutual responsibility model that will combat the fears of both the minority and the majority.

AN ILLUSTRATION FROM MARRIAGE

Let us imagine a horrible marriage in which the husband treats his wife brutally. He physically abuses and dominates her. He has multiple extramarital affairs. His conduct humiliates his wife. Finally the wife has had enough. She tells him that if he does not change, then the marriage is over. After thinking it through, the husband decides that he wants to keep his marriage. He tells his wife that he will not abuse her or cheat on her again. What will become of the marriage if the husband keeps his promise?

One possible outcome is that the marriage improves, but only marginally. The man never genuinely repented of his sins. He only agreed not to conduct himself in that way any longer. Has he really had a change of heart, or has he reformed because it is convenient for him? If he has had a change of heart, then his new actions are based on internal convictions that will help insure that he keeps his promises. The wife can have some assurance that he is acting for her betterment and not just because it is good for him right now. If he is acting only from convenience, then his wife must live in uncertainty because he may go back to his old behaviors if he can get away with it. The wife's fears will prevent the couple from developing the sort of trust and intimacy they need to rebuild their marriage.

There is another possible outcome if the man changes his ways. Perhaps he does repent of his sins. He holds himself more accountable to his wife so she can be confident that he is not cheating. He goes out of his way to show her respect and to refrain from any kind of abuse. However, the wife is human; she too can sin. She can be tempted to use the new situation to dominate the relationship. She may make unreasonable requests so that he becomes her servant. Because of his previous behavior, the husband is unable to confront the wife with her own selfishness, and the relationship becomes stilted. The husband begins to fear that his wife will use his previous sins to avoid her own responsibilities. Once again fear prevents the couple from gaining the intimacy and trust their marriage needs in order to thrive. This time it is the husband's fear which hampers the marriage.

In my analogy, the husband represents whites, and the wife represents people of color. The husband's abuse represents the historic abuse people of color have suffered at the hands of whites. The wife's demand for change represents the civil rights movement. The husband's decision to change represents the resulting civil rights legislation. But where we go from there depends on how we handle our fears. The wife fears that the husband will not be true to his word. She is not sure whether he has truly repented or is only treating her well now because of circumstances. Likewise, people of color are fearful of the possible future actions of majority group members. Are whites serious about dealing with racial injustice, or are they merely mouthing words to ease their conscience? Are whites truly willing to change their ways, or will they only do what is convenient? Racial minorities' fears can prevent the growth of healthy race relations. But notice that the husband's fear can also prevent reconciliation. Will the wife abuse her new position of authority to conceal her own shortcomings? Will she seek revenge with her new ability to shame her husband? Whites fear that people of color will use accusations of racism to conceal their own sins or to gain an unfair advantage over whites. Just as fear can prevent the development of a healthy marriage, it can impede on the possibility of righteous race relations.

There is a third possible alternative. The husband and wife can begin to talk about their fears of each other. When the husband hears his wife's fears, he can adjust his actions to lessen her apprehension. He can make restitution for the sins both of them agree he has committed. He can show his wife that his change goes down to his very core. The wife can also listen to her husband's fears that she will use his past sins against him. She can acknowledge that she is also a sinner, and she can listen to him when he confronts her with her own sins. She can examine her demands to see if they are based on legitimate needs or on her own selfishness. I make no claim to be a marriage counselor, but it is obvious to me that only by entering into honest dialogue and acknowledging their sin nature can this couple overcome the previous abuses of the husband and restore intimacy to their marriage.[2]

In the above example, the relationship was healed only when both the husband and the wife were able to confront and face each other's fears. Likewise, only when both white Christians and Christians of color acknowledge white privilege and the race card will we see how our fears and sin nature inhibit our ability to overcome our terrible racial history.

We cannot overcome our history by ignoring the capacity of whites and nonwhites to sin. The secular models either ignore how whites have benefited from racism or they ignore how people of color use accusations of racism to further their own self-interest. That is why these models will never be adequate to deal with the spiritual dimensions of racism. Our fear toward those of other races is linked to our conscious and subconscious knowledge that their sin nature can operate against us. A Christian mutual responsibility model recognizes that it is only when we acknowledge our sin nature that we will be able to deal with racism.

OVERCOMING OUR FEARS

My illustration from marriage can be faulted for several reasons. Relationships between groups are not the same as a marriage relationship; a man-woman relationship contains a romantic element not present in race relations; people alive today did not commit those heinous racial sins symbolized by the man's adultery. All analogies eventually break down. But my illustration holds up in a crucial area. In both cases, fear about what the other party will do threatens to make a bad situation worse. Fear is destructive, whether we experience it in interpersonal relationships or in intergroup contact.

Our society lacks safe places to talk about race. The absence is obvious in my race/ethnicity classes. Powerful political forces seek to shape the discourse in academia. Students perceive that they will be judged for what they say and that there are real consequences to these judgments. In an environment where people fear judgment, they will allow their fears to control them. A judgmental environment is embedded in contemporary academia, and it produces the politically correct conversations that fail to ease racial strife. As long as certain forces have the power to punish whites who seem insensitive to people of color, or to punish people of color who seem to complain too much, honest dialogue on college campuses will be limited.

The lack of safe places to discuss racial issues in the secular world means that Christians should work harder to create safe places in our churches. People will be able to explore genuine answers instead of parroting secular models. Honest dialogue in a Christian setting is vital since our faith teaches us the role of human depravity in the development of racism. We will understand not only that people of other races may be insensitive to our perspective on racial issues, but that we may be insensitive to their perspective as well. When we humbly realize the implications of human depravity, we can work toward creating the safe spaces necessary for racial healing.[3]

In the creation of safe spaces we can rid ourselves of the fears that drive racial mistrust. In safe spaces majority and minority group members can take the potentially costly chances necessary to deal with racial alienation. Majority group members can overcome their fears that racial minorities will take advantage of their repentance. Minorities can overcome their fears that majority group members will dismiss racial concerns once minorities have extended forgiveness.

HOW CAN WE CREATE A SAFE ENVIRONMENT?

Christians have an advantage over the secular world in creating a safe environment to talk about race. We understand the reality of human depravity. Secular philosophies have developed the idea that humans are perfectible.[4] Those who push human perfectibility focus on education to improve humanity. The argument has been made that education is the best way to deal with racism.[5] I personally have nothing against education. I am an educator myself. However, I do not believe that education will solve our racial problems.[6] The use of education to promote ideas of tolerance, colorblindness and reconciliation inhibits the ability of our educational institutions to become safe places where we can discuss racial issues. If anything, they become less safe because anyone who challenges the dominant ideology will face resistance and penalties from school administrators.

The mutual responsibility model creates an atmosphere in which people of all races are free to explore their fears without undue judgment. Christians know that we are not perfectible this side of heaven (Romans 3:10-18, 23). We can and should become more sanctified in our actions, which means that we should try to eradicate racism and racial alienation. But we should not expect others to be perfect. We should be humble enough to recognize that we ourselves are not perfect. As imperfect sinners, all we can do is seek to help each other and help ourselves overcome the poison of sin in the form of racism. We have no basis for pride in the way we deal with racism and no basis for judging others. We should do our best to hold others accountable for their sins (Matthew 18:15-18) but never with a haughty attitude (Galatians 6:1).

People of color often fear that interracial dialogue will be nothing but rehashing old issues and that little concrete action will result. But this conversation should not end in mere talk. We must take action to validate the concerns of those with whom we talk.

Chris Rice, a white Christian, participated in the dialogue on racial reconciliation in Mississippi. He reacted to African Americans' concerns about white paternalism by taking a back seat to the emerging black Christian leaders.[7] Later those same black leaders recognized Rice's leadership abilities and placed him back in a leadership role. Rice's ability to listen and take action on what he heard allowed the African Americans to trust him, and racial healing became possible.

What would such dialogue look like in our churches? Majority group members would become less judgmental of the complaints of people of color and would look for the validity of their complaints. Majority group members may not agree with minorities on all issues, but they would take those issues seriously. On the other hand, racial minorities would be more restrained in how they express their concerns, because they would know that their own sin nature seduces them to exaggerate their concerns so they can gain power. If someone tries to play the race card, then people of color, not whites, would call the player on the carpet.

Such conversations can become reality in our churches if we adjust our attitude toward those who disagree with us. We must be open to others who do not see the issue of race as we do. We must be quick to listen and slow to speak (James 1:19). More than ever we must take seriously the biblical command not to judge others (Matthew 7:1).

While every Christian has a role to play, our leaders must be especially willing to work to create safe zones. We must begin to teach about human depravity as a major contributor to racial strife. It is particularly important that we admit human depravity in our own racial group and not just focus on using the concept to condemn those of other races. Christian leaders must condemn any ideology that only enhances racial power at the expense of other racial groups. Far too often we hear black liberals or the white religious right demonized from pulpits. Legitimate critiques of any group are welcome, but hateful rhetoric that dehumanizes others must be opposed. We cannot develop godly relationships with those of different races if we see those who disagree with us as enemies to be conquered. The mutual responsibility model compels us to look for allies, not rant against enemies. Jesus has taught us to put others before ourselves (Luke 14:7-14). We can become Christians who lead the way to finding real solutions to racial issues, not Christians who follow the latest secular fad.

LET ME START WITH MYSELF

If I call Christians to be honest about their own issues of racism, then it is only fair that I lead by example and not merely by exhortation. I want to end this chapter in the same way I began my first book. I want those who read this book to know that I do not claim to have ultimate knowledge about how to solve racism. I too am a sinner who is struggling to find his way. I want to share the moment that I discovered that racism was not just the other person's problem but mine as well.

> During my last year in Austin I lived in the northeastern part of the city in an interracial neighborhood. One day while I was watching the news, I heard that there had been a police shooting. While not an everyday occurrence, this was not unusual in Austin; however, my interest was piqued when I found out that it was in northeast Austin. The story really got my attention when the news reporter mentioned a street that was very close to where I lived. Then I listened intently to the details of the story.
>
> It seemed that a man had been harassing a woman and had been driven off earlier by the police. He was told not to come back to that address. Unfortunately he did not listen and came back later that night. The woman called the police and when they showed up, the man produced what appeared to them to be a gun. The man was shot several times and killed. Afterward the police discovered that what they thought was a real gun was only a toy weapon.

As I listened to this story, there was one overwhelming thought in my mind: *I hope that guy was not black*. You see, if the man was black then I would wonder if racism was involved in the incident. Would the police have used such excessive force if the man had been white? Not only would I wonder if racism might have been a factor, but I would anticipate the various African American political and religious groups beginning to place the label of racism on the incident. This was a reasonable fear after seeing the damage that similar incidents had done to cities such as Los Angeles and Miami. The city of Austin would be faced with a whole new round of racial introspection, not all of which would be helpful to the process of reconciliation. Later I found out that the assailant was white and all of these fears were put aside.

Even as I was putting these fears aside, however, a new set of fears began to crop up in my mind. I began to think about my desire that a man who had been killed have a particular skin color. To put my dilemma in perspective I imagined someone like David Duke wishing that same sort of thing I had. What would you think if you knew Duke had heard of a police shooting and said, "Well, I hope they shot a black man"? Images of white robes and burning crosses would probably cross your mind. Was I any better? Is not hoping that an individual who has been killed is not black roughly the same as hoping that he is white? In horror I began to examine myself. Was I as guilty of racism as Duke? Perhaps my racism was merely different in degree from Duke's but not in kind.

I began to try to find ways to justify my thinking. After all, we know that someone like Duke would make his statement out of disrespect for the personhood of blacks. My thought was in response to the potential problems an act of racism would bring to my city. Surely my motives were more pure than those of someone like Duke. This excuse did not satisfy me for long. It may be true that I was responding to the societal situation around me; however, the grand wizard of the Klan could say the same thing. We have all seen pictures of white children at Klan rallies. When they grow up, they are just living by the lessons that society has taught them. In their minds, they are as certain that the mixing of the races is problematic to society as I was that a surge of protests after a racial shooting would have been. In both circumstances we are reacting to fears caused by society and thus allowing the development of racism.

This brings out a very important point about racism. We live in a racist society. Racism is not found only way down south or in certain neighborhoods. Unfortunately the phenomenon of racism is part of what makes America what it is. It is in our history and our culture. I am not trying to sound like some sort of unpatriotic radical; I am merely telling the truth. We cannot change a reality until we are willing to acknowledge the presence of that reality. I have to admit that racism is as much a part of my subculture as it is part of David Duke's. Racism is in David Duke. It is in the skinheads. It is in the black nationalists. But more important, at least from my viewpoint, racism is in me. The society has taught me to be racist and I have learned those lessons well. I cannot ignore the realities of racism in our society, so sometimes, in reaction, I act or think in racist ways. I want to think that racism is something that is only found in those groups or individuals that we tend to think of as bigots. But now I am forced to be honest. It is in me as well.[8]

What Would a Christian Solution Look Like?

Can Christians offer unique solutions to racism in keeping with our faith? I have already discussed the ideas of corporate repentance and forgiveness. I believe that corporate repentance and forgiveness are enough to make a change in American race relations. But because of human depravity, we must go further. A truly Christian solution will drive us to look beyond what we can gain to how we can love and give to those of different races. When both whites and nonwhites take seriously the idea of putting others' interests above their own, then we will see a genuine Christian remedy for racial problems.

What would our society look like if we were able to incorporate a Christian solution to racial problems? To be honest, I cannot say. I do not believe that any society has incorporated a truly Christian solution for intergroup strife. In this final chapter I will do my best to create a picture of what a Christian solution might look like. My hope is to encourage us to work toward that solution and to give us a target to aim for.

A NEW RELATIONSHIP

Different models offer distinct visions of what a racially harmonious society would look like. The colorblindness model sees a society where skin color is no more important than eye color. The white responsibility model sees a society where racial minorities finally get their due. By contrast, the mutual responsibility model envisions a society where we have healed our damaged racial relationships.

Repentance and forgiveness, so important to any interpersonal relationships, are also vital to racial relationships. They can help correct previously dysfunctional relations. But they do not help us maintain a healthy relationship. We need other Christian principles to take us from healing our historic racial sickness to maintaining healthy relationships with each other. If we can get a sense of what truly egalitarian race relationships look like at an interpersonal level, we will understand what they look like at a structural level. To illustrate, I will look at my own interracial marriage.

Both Sherelyn and I are fallen creatures who are selfish, and our faults come through in our marriage. Most of the struggles in our marriage have nothing to do with racial issues but instead are the same relational struggles that all married couples face. However, because we are an interracial couple, we have to deal with racial issues as well as other issues. Sherelyn is not free to ignore my concerns as a member of a racial minority. If she did, it would eventually harm our relationship beyond repair. Likewise, I am not free to play the race card just because it is available, since it would damage Sherelyn's ability to trust me.

In the first chapter of this book I mentioned how I feel when I hear car doors being locked as I approach or even as cars pass me. Early in our marriage I noticed that Sherelyn would lock the car doors whenever she stopped at a stoplight and any men were close by. Her habit became a source of tension between us. For her, it was not a racial issue but a safety issue. While I believed her when she claimed that she had no racial motivations, I could not dismiss my own experience. If Sherelyn had adopted a colorblindness perspective, she could have ignored my concerns. Her reaction would have made me more defensive and resentful toward her. Either we would have continually argued about the issue or I would have stopped trusting her to look out for my good.

We developed a compromise. We agreed that Sherelyn can lock the car doors before we drive or if there is no one else around. However, she no longer locks the car door as we drive by a man of color. She will wait until we are far enough away from him that he cannot hear the doors locking. This eliminates the insult of the sound of car doors locking yet allows her to feel secure as she drives. The key is that she had to listen to my concern and take it seriously before we could find a solution.

European Americans are not the only ones who damage race relations. The mutual responsibility model recognizes that racial minorities are also quite adept at injuring our relations with majority group members. We often hurt ourselves by playing the race card for our own gain, not to point out a legitimate concern.

Early in our marriage we went through a common struggle over household duties. What made our situation unique was that I had an extra card to play. When Sherelyn requested of me what I thought was too much, I could always accuse her of treating me like a slave. When a black man accuses his white wife of treating him like a slave, we are not talking about a normal argument. He is using the race card to get his way without having to go through the normal marital process of negotiations.

Because I played the race card, Sherelyn stopped trusting me when I made other claims of racial bias. She saw that I used racial charges to unfairly get my way. Over time I have learned to argue in a way that does not misuse the race card, and I have regained Sherelyn's trust. Does that mean that I can never bring up racial issues in our marriage? No. Remember that I brought her habit of locking car doors to her attention. But the door locking was a legitimate racial issue; I was not trying to gain anything from her. She could respect my concerns about the car door locking only because I had stopped playing the race card.

For marriages to work, the marital partners cannot think only of their own needs. They have to take into account the needs of the marriage partner. The two examples above illustrate that for Sherelyn and me to deal with racial issues in our marriage, we have to let go of our own desires and consider the other person's concerns. Likewise, healthy racial relationships cannot be maintained unless people from different races are willing to take seriously the concerns of those who are racially different.

The mutual responsibility model is a Christian solution by which whites become so concerned about people of color that they listen to what they say without dismissing them as overly sensitive. Likewise the mutual responsibility model will result in people of color refusing to allow racial charges to be leveled against whites unless legitimate racial wrongs have been done.

A REAL-WORLD EXAMPLE: AFFIRMATIVE ACTION

I would be remiss if I left the mutual responsibility model at a theoretical level and did not try to envision what it would look like in our society. My explanation will be somewhat hypothetical since I do not believe that there is now any good example of the implementation of the mutual responsibility model. However, by looking at a real racial issue and applying what I believe is a Christian perspective, we can find insight about how to approach racial issues as I believe Christ would have us approach them.

The issue I will use as an example is affirmative action. It is probably one of the most controversial issues in our society. If we can determine a Christian approach to this issue, then we can see how the mutual responsibility model would address other racial issues.

The concept of affirmative action dates back to 1967 when President Lyndon Johnson first used the term concerning the enforcement of anti-discrimination measures for government agencies and businesses working for the government. His order not only forbade discrimination because of race but also required those agencies and business contractors to develop goals and timetables as targets for hiring racial minorities and women. These programs became much more widespread during the 1970s, especially on college campuses. Recent court cases have challenged affirmative action programs.

Generally whites oppose affirmative action more than people of color do.[1] This should not come as a surprise. Affirmative action helps people of color overcome the effects of historic racism. It allows people of color to make social, educational and material gains, sometimes at the expense of majority group members. Naturally, European Americans are not going to favor such action, while racial minorities are going to support it. Both are normal human responses because of the nature of human depravity. We tend to favor what helps us and resist what may harm us, regardless of whether it is more beneficial or harmful to society as a whole. No wonder there has been so much conflict over affirmative action.

Given the history of affirmative action and the controversy surrounding it, we can ask whether a Christian approach would support it or resist it. In the mutual responsibility model, that is the wrong question. Rather we should ask whether or not this program serves the interest of all races. We should ask this question regardless of our race. Majority group members must honestly look at whether this program helps the legitimate needs of people of color. They must listen to the historic and contemporary grievances of people of color against our society. I believe that if whites listen to those grievances with an open heart, they will understand the needs that affirmative action meets. They still may not agree with the program, but if they accept the mutual responsibility model, I think they will at least offer something else in its place.

People of color must also become sensitive to the needs and perceptions of European Americans. Our problems are not all directly related to the presence and influence of majority group members. Remedies for our racial struggles can sometimes overcorrect the problems they were designed to fix. It is indeed possible for racial justice to become racial injustice, and whites can be exploited in the process.

We minorities must constantly review our motives to make sure that in our discussions about affirmative action we avoid playing the race card, unless we are indeed talking about some form of racism. If we accept the mutual responsibility model, we cannot claim that we have no responsibility for what happens; we must acknowledge how we contribute to our own failings. We examine ourselves, not so we can let whites off the hook, but so we do not put them on that hook when it is not justified. If we truly love and care for our white Christian brothers and sisters, we will not want them to feel guilty over something which is really our responsibility.

There is no single all-encompassing Christian answer for whether we should have affirmative action. There are likely some aspects of the program we should keep and others we should reform or even discard.[2] Affirmative action aims to help correct some of the effects of historic and institutional racism. I think we can make a valid argument that something like affirmative action is necessary after centuries of abuse. However, the form it should take and how long it should last are problematic questions. We risk adopting a program that is either too weak to provide real racial relief for people of color or so powerful that it overcorrects for the problems it was designed to solve.

I believe there is a middle ground that would be beneficial for our society, but human depravity persuades us to answer these questions in a way that benefits our own group. As long as we are trapped by the sin of selfishness, we will never find the middle ground.[3]

The Christian solution is not a direct answer but an attitude which leads to the correct answer. It is not unlike the attitudes of both partners in a good marriage. Both partners take into account the interests and needs of the other so their relationship thrives. A marriage in which one partner must acquiesce all the time is not healthy.

Corporate repentance and forgiveness are part of the mutual responsibility solution. Whites are not going to trust racial minorities if they suspect that minorities will use racial issues against them. Racial minorities will not trust whites unless they perceive that whites genuinely care about their racial concerns and show real repentance. As we grow from the initial stages of repentance and forgiveness, we will find answers that take into account the needs of those of all races.

We can do this. We can begin to build racial relationships where one group is not always victimized. When we do so, the rest of society will marvel at our Christian witness. It is our responsibility as Christians to provide this witness and to learn to die to ourselves as we pursue Christian solutions to racism.

WHERE DO WE BEGIN?

How do we start to display the mutual responsibility model to the rest of society? How do we start to develop the solutions that our society so desperately needs? I believe we are at the beginning of the process and no one has complete answers about how we are going to overcome racial problems. But let me offer a few suggestions to help us think about how to facilitate a Christian understanding of racial issues.

Multiracial churches. I was fortunate to have the opportunity to work on the first national research project that examined interracial churches. I have written two books exploring why interracial churches are important[4] and what churches can do to become multiracial or to maintain their racial diversity.[5] According to this research, less than 8 percent of our churches are multiracial.[6] Is it not a shame that in a country as racially diverse as ours, less than one out of every ten churches is multiracial? One of the best ways to heal racial strife is to fellowship with Christians of different races. Multiracial churches must deal with the various ways that people of different races perceive racial issues.[7] The existence of multiracial churches provides a powerful witness to a racially segregated society.

Successful multiracial churches share certain characteristics, including racially diverse leadership, inclusive worship and adaptability.[8] These characteristics help Christians learn more about how to love each other. Let us examine one of them: inclusive worship. By that I mean worship which is inclusive of various racial cultures. While not all successful multiracial churches I studied have inclusive worship, most of them did because it was important for them to find ways for members of all racial groups to feel included. Some churches used songs from different cultures in each service (for example black gospel, a traditional European hymn, a song in Spanish) while others devoted entire worship services to a particular racial tradition (for example an Asian-style worship service one Sunday, a service in a Latino style the next Sunday). Despite differences in how they accomplish inclusive worship, successful multiracial churches regularly include cultural elements of different races. Inclusive worship calms the multiculturalist's fears about minority groups losing their culture, but in a way which does not overly glorify minority cultures.

I believe that it is important for churches to put a priority on the development of multiracial ministries. Fortunately many denominational leaders are doing this. Yet the average church worker still is clueless about the power of these ministries and may even resist the change. A great challenge of the twenty-first-century church is to find ways to encourage the growth of multiracial Christian institutions.

Social networks. People of our own race tend to make up our social networks.[9] It happens not because of some racist conspiracy but because we tend to take the path of least resistance. In a society as racially segregated as the United States, we naturally have friends of our own race. Many people will protest that they do have friends of different races. But research has shown, at least for whites,[10] that having a few friends of different races in one's social network does not significantly alter one's outlook on racial issues.[11] For racial perceptions to be influenced by interracial friendships, we must be involved in social networks that are thoroughly multiracial.[12] Christians should not think that because they have a friend or two of a different race, they understand people of that race.[13]

Our vision must be proactive rather than reactive. Christians must make the effort to go out of their way to gain friends of different races. We will do this not to appear politically correct but because we want to overcome the old animosities between us. Most of us would be surprised, if we looked at our workplaces, schools and social circles, to see how many people of different races there are around us.[14] Diversifying our social networks is a Christian way to help heal racial strife in our society.

A good friend of mine has chosen to move his family into a racially mixed neighborhood. Such a move is not easy in a residentially segregated society, but he is committed to developing relationships with those of other races, and he wants his children to develop interracial friendships. Here is an especially powerful way to overcome racial barriers. Research indicates that Americans who develop racially inclusive social networks early in life are likely to maintain those networks throughout their lives.[15] We should go out of our way to find friends of different races, not only for ourselves but for our children and for the next generation of believers.

Political activism. Political activism is a difficult issue for Christians to tackle. The political racial divide in our society is well established.[16] European Americans are more prone to support Republicans, while people of color are more prone to support Democrats. Among evangelicals the divide is even greater. White evangelicals are more likely than other whites to support Republicans, and black evangelicals are more likely than other blacks to support Democrats.[17] It appears that our Christian faith only intensifies political differences between the races.

Abortion is one of the big issues which drives white Christians' loyalty to the Republican Party.[18] Beyond the research that indicates this fact, I have talked with many white Christians who cannot think of voting for a prochoice candidate. Because the majority of Democratic office holders are prochoice, these white Christians vote Republican. Since I am prolife myself, I understand their desire to stand up for innocent life. At the same time, concerns about racial justice drive the loyalties of people of color. Because Republicans generally resist racially based programs such as affirmative action and hate-crimes legislation, people of color doubt that Republicans will do whatever it takes to provide them with racial justice. Their uncertainty has led them into the arms of the Democrats, who are more willing to support multicultural and race-based solutions. I too have questioned whether the Republican Party is willing to produce real solutions to racism.

Neither the Democrats nor the Republicans are God's political party. There are solid Bible-believing Christians in both parties. I believe that both parties depart from God's perfect will on some issues and are closer to his truth on other issues. The hostility between white Christians and Christians of color is not ordained by God; it is a natural result of our depravity. The enemy uses our political differences to keep us apart. We must think carefully about political activism that we do in the name of Christianity, such as supporting supposedly Christian candidates, inviting political candidates to speak at our churches and passing out voter guides. We must consider whether our actions will help or hinder racial reconciliation.

Then should Christians refrain from participating in the political process? Should we participate only if we do not identify ourselves as Christians? I do not believe we have to show that much restraint. I do believe we have to reconsider how we participate in the political process. For example, Christians may question the faith of those who do not vote for a certain political party. I have heard white Christian Republicans make this accusation of Christian Democrats. The result is that they drive away minority Christians who are Democrats. Racial minorities may be prolife[19] but disagree with the Republican Party on issues such as health care, defense spending or gun control. It is one thing to support one's own political party. It is quite another to accuse members of the other party of being unchristian.

Christians of color are not innocent of playing politics in a way that fosters racial alienation. I have seen minority Christians demonize Republicans in a way that is frankly unchristlike. It is one thing to disagree with a party's platform; it is quite another to accuse the members of that party of racism. Here is another example of playing the race card. Why would white Christian Republicans with legitimate concerns about the lives of the unborn want to seek out relationships with those who call them racist? Christians of color should be careful about throwing out accusations of racism when what is really occurring is political disagreement or the clash of two views of morality.

I am not saying that we should discard our political ideals. There are Christians in both parties who have arrived at their convictions through careful thought and application of their Christian faith. But I urge all of us to pursue our Christian interests in ways that do not dehumanize believers of the other party. Perhaps we can even learn something from those in another party. We will not build a multiracial Christianity by yelling insults at each other but by learning how to disagree on the nonessentials. I believe that most political issues are ultimately nonessentials when compared with the foundations of our faith. If we can get along with each other in the political sphere, we will show the world that political pressures need not divide us.

Christian academic institutions. Many of our Christian academic institutions are reproducing the mistakes of the past. For example, research done by my colleagues indicates that the concept of colorblindness dominates at one prominent Christian college. Because of the way colorblindness plays itself out on this campus, racial minorities feel unwanted and feel that their concerns are not being heard.[20] No wonder Christian colleges are less likely than secular schools to attract students of color.[21]

Christian colleges' failure to promote racial reconciliation is particularly distressing because they are the source of our future Christian leaders. If there is any place where we need to implement the Christian mutual responsibility model, it is in our universities and seminaries. Why not initiate campus dialogue in which white college students hear the pain of people of color and understand why they have so much racial distrust? We can do this through carefully constructed diversity courses, competent speakers of color and the organization of racially diverse small groups. Such efforts will allow European American Christians to learn about the racial pain of people of color, help people of color express their hurt, provide a forum where corporate repentance can take place and encourage students of color to forgive and to release any grudges they continue to hold.

We should also think about the responsibilities of Christian professors. It is not enough that Christian professors avoid overt racial discrimination or harmful racial stereotypes. We need academic Christian men and women to engage in discourse and research about how the body of Christ can be a healing force in society. The mutual responsibility model is only a foundation on which other Christian scholars can build to develop a Christian solution to racism. We need Christian professors to reach beyond the secular models of the world and find Christian models to move us beyond the standards of this society.[22] Solid arguments and research from professors on Christian campuses will go a long way to show Christian students how seriously we should take the problem of racism. Fortunately there are professors in Christian colleges and seminaries who are taking up this call. We need more of them if we are going to bring about long-term change.

AN INCOMPLETE PICTURE

My suggestions paint an incomplete picture of what the mutual responsibility model will ultimately look like, but right now it is the only picture I have. You have an opportunity to help me produce a more complete picture of racial reconciliation. If you are willing to put aside your own group's interests and listen to the concerns of others, then you will have a part in creating that picture. If you are open to repenting and forgiving, then you will have a part in creating that picture. If you are willing to be accountable to those of different races and learn from them, then you will have a part in creating that picture. If you are willing to develop a teachable spirit, then you will have a part in creating that picture.

But if you are unwilling to do these things, then your picture is already painted. You can see it in the insufficient results of the colorblindness, Anglo-conformity, multiculturalist and white responsibility models. Your painting may have good elements, but it will lack critical details. I want to paint a new picture that reveals to other members of the body of Christ and to the world that my God is not too small to deal with racial hostility.

Are you willing to help me to paint that picture? I do not pretend to have all the answers or to know every step of the path to get there. I will need to learn from others as we walk this path together. I believe it is the narrow path that God has put before those who want to set aside their own desires and find his will (Matthew 7:13-14). We must abandon the broad path which has led so many Christians and non-Christians into inadequate solutions. Let us work together to find the path of faith that leads to true racial reconciliation.

Notes

Introduction

[1] George Gallup Jr. and D. Michael Lindsay, *Surveying the Religious Landscape: Trends in U.S. Beliefs* (Harrisburg, Penn.: Morehouse, 1999), pp. 102-5; B. R. Hertel and M. Hughes, "Religious Affiliation, Attendance, and Support for 'Pro-Family' Issues in the United States," *Social Forces* 65, no. 3 (1987): 858-82; J. Strickler and N. L. Danigelis, "Changing Frameworks in Attitudes Toward Abortion," *Sociological Forum* 17, no. 2 (2002): 187-201; G.-z. Wang and M. D. Buffalo, "Social and Cultural Determinants of Attitudes Toward Abortion: A Test of Reiss' Hypotheses," *Social Science Journal* 41, no. 1 (2004): 93-105.

[2] Naturally those of other faiths may find reasons within their religious traditions to support or oppose abortion. An exploration of their reasons is beyond the scope of this discussion.

[3] Lee Epstein and Joseph F. Kobylka, *The Supreme Court and Legal Change* (Chapel Hill: University of North Carolina Press, 1992); J. H. Evans, "Polarization in Abortion Attitudes in U.S. Religious Traditions, 1972-1998," *Sociological Forum* 17, no. 3 (2002): 397-422; Kristin Luker, *Abortion and the Politics of Motherhood* (Berkeley: University of California Press, 1985).

[4] Brian C. Anderson, "Secular Europe, Religious America," *Public Interest* 155 (2004): 143-58; L. Voye, "Secularization in a Context of Advanced Modernity," *Sociology of Religion* 60, no. 3 (1999): 275-88.

[5] Other issues of structural inequality, such as sexism and classism, were not addressed at this Bible study either. The neglect of racism in the Bible study was likely due to the tendency of white evangelical Christians to focus on individual morality while neglecting issues of structural morality.

[6] Because I am not a trained theologian, my discussion of theological issues will be less thorough than some readers may hope. I do not want the discussion to get bogged down by theological debates. Occasionally I will relegate theological issues to endnotes.

[7]This assertion is based on realized eschatology rather than on dispensational theology. Realized eschatology holds Christians responsible for improving society, while the traditional dispensational view argues that there is nothing we can do to make things better until Christ returns and the kingdom of God comes. Under the dispensational view it is useless to try to heal our hurting race relations since only the return of Christ will bring about complete healing. I do believe that we must wait for the kingdom of God before we experience full reconciliation of people who are divided by human sin, but we still have a responsibility to confront societal sin whenever we can.

[8]Not only would we be able to witness to our fellow Americans, but we would also witness to the rest of world. The United States is not the only country with hostile intergroup relations. If we can demonstrate ways to overcome racial hostility, then we will be able to comment on other hostile relations in the world, such as intergroup conflicts in Sudan or Israel.

[9]George Yancey, *Beyond Black and White: Reflections on Racial Reconciliation* (Grand Rapids: Baker, 1996).

[10]R. Anstey, "A Re-Interpretation of the Abolition of the British Slave Trade, 1806-1807," *The English Historical Review* 87, no. 343 (1972): 304-32; G. E. Finnie, "The Antislavery Movement in the Upper South Before 1840," *The Journal of Southern History* 35, no. 3 (1969): 319-42; A. E. Martin, "Pioneer Anti-Slavery Press," *The Mississippi Valley Historical Review* 2, no. 4 (1916): 509-28.

[11]R. Bogin and Jean F. Yellin, introduction, and A. Swerdlow, "Abolition's Conservative Sisters: The Ladies' New York City Anti-Slavery Societies, 1834-1840," in *The Abolition Sisterhood: Women's Political Culture in Antebellum America,* ed. Jean F. Yellin and John C. Van Horne (Ithaca, N.Y.: Cornell University Press, 1994).

[12]Mark A. Noll, *A History of Christianity in the United States and Canada* (Grand Rapids: Eerdmans, 1992); Marjorie S. Wheeler, ed., *One Woman One Vote: Rediscovering the Woman Suffrage Movement* (Portland, Ore.: New Sage, 1995).

[13] For example, Christian church leaders developed the idea that women had the right to control their households. Christian women argued that they were unable to do so because of alcohol and other moral abuses (Nancy Woloch, *Women and the American Experience: A Concise History,* 2nd ed. [Boston: McGraw-Hill, 2002]). Women argued that the government would better control these moral abuses if women were able to influence the public sector. With such an argument, leaders such as Frances Willard and Annie Wittenmyer were able to justify the vote for women in a traditional, patriarchal society. To give women the right to vote gave them power to control their households, which Christians saw as a female responsibility.

Chapter 1: Two Views of Racism
[1]Michael O. Emerson and Christian Smith, *Divided by Faith: Evangelical Religion and*

the Problem of Race in America (Oxford: Oxford University Press, 2000), pp. 88-91.

[2]Andrew J. Cherlin, *Marriage, Divorce, Remarriage* (Cambridge, Mass.: Harvard University Press, 1992); James A. Sweet and Larry L. Bumpass, *American Families and Households* (New York: Russell Sage Foundation, 1987).

[3]A. M. DeBlassie and R. R. DeBlassie, "Education of Hispanic Youth: A Cultural Lag," *Adolescence* 31, no. 121 (1996): 205-16; Jacqueline J. Irvine, *Black Students and School Failure: Policies, Practices, and Prescriptions* (Westport, Conn.: Praeger, 1991); Jonathan Kozol, *Savage Inequalities: Children in America's Schools* (New York: Crown, 1991); Nancy L. Maxwell, "The Effects on Black-White Wage Differences in the Quantity and Quality of Education," *Industrial and Labor Relations Review* 47, no. 2 (1994): 249-65.

[4]Emerson and Smith, *Divided by Faith,* p. 97.

[5]Ibid.

[6]Mark R. McMinn, *Why Sin Matters: The Surprising Relationship Between Our Sin and God's Grace* (Wheaton, Ill.: Tyndale House, 2004), pp. 72-73. If we need any scriptural support for this point, we need only look at Jesus' instruction about pulling the log out of our own eye before trying to remove the speck in the other person's eye (Matthew 7:3-5) or his parable about the servant whose debt was forgiven but who refused to forgive the smaller debt of his fellow servant (Matthew 18:23-35).

[7]In chapter five I point out how work by Peggy McIntosh on white privilege supports this assertion. She argues that whites do not easily recognize the advantages their race brings them, in part because the privileges are not overt and in part because recognizing them would force them to do something about institutional racism.

[8]I use the term "racial reconciliation" as a more spiritualized term because of the scriptural connotations of reconciliation. Some have opposed the use of the term "racial reconciliation" because it implies repairing relationships that once were healthy. Critics rightly point out that we have never had healthy race relations in the United States. I take such considerations seriously. However, I am looking at a more scriptural understanding of reconciliation. A biblical understanding of reconciliation means healing the broken relationship between God and human beings. Likewise, Christians talk about the healing of broken race relations. Thus I do not hesitate to talk about racial reconciliation, because reconciliation in a fallen world is one of the tasks Christians are called to accomplish.

Chapter 2: Colorblindness

[1]Eduardo Bonilla-Silva, *White Supremacy and Racism in the Post-Civil Rights Era* (Boulder, Colo.: Lynne Rienner Publishers, 2001); Leslie G. Carr, *Color-Blind Racism* (Thousand Oaks, Calif.: Sage Publications, 1997); H. Dalton, "Failing to See," in *White Privilege: Essential Readings on the Other Side of Racism,* ed. Paula S. Rothenberg (New York: Worth, 2002), pp. 15-18; C. Gallagher, "Racial Redistricting:

Expanding the Boundaries of Whiteness," in *The Multiracial Movement: The Politics of Color* (New York: State University of New York, 2003); D. O. Sears, "Symbolic Racism," in *Eliminating Racism*, ed. Phyllis A. Katz and Dalmas A. Taylor (New York: Plenum, 1988); J. Sidanius, F. Pratto and Lawrence Bobo, "Racism, Conservatism, Affirmative Action, and Intellectual Sophistication: A Matter of Principled Conservatism or Group Dominance?" *Journal of Personality and Social Psychology* 70, no. 3 (1996): 476-90.

[2]Bonilla-Silva, *White Supremacy*; Carr, *Color-Blind Racism*; Sidanius et al., "Racism, Conservatism."

[3]Proponents of colorblindness may contend that racial discrimination cannot be regulated since it is not the place of the government to legislate social concerns. On the one hand, this convinces some supporters of colorblindness to oppose legislation that seeks to encourage racial residential integration. On the other hand, the value of colorblindness means that individuals who choose to live in another residential area only because they want to stay away from people of other races are morally wrong. The key to the colorblindness perspective on social issues is that individuals are free to choose what they want to do, but the right choice is to ignore race.

[4]*Jim Crow* refers to the situation of legal segregation in the southern United States in the early twentieth century. In *Plessy v. Ferguson* the Supreme Court ruled that racial separation was legal as long as facilities were equal for whites and blacks, commonly called the *separate but equal* rule. Of course blacks were not given equal facilities, and *separate but equal* was used to insure that blacks would continue to suffer disenfranchisement.

[5]Martin Luther King Jr., *Why We Can't Wait* (New York: New American Library, 2000).

[6]David Horowitz, *Left Illusions: An Intellectual Odyssey* (Dallas: Spence, 2003).

[7]Dinesh D'Souza, *The End of Racism: Principles for a Multiracial Society* (New York: Free Press, 1996).

[8]Ward Connerly, *Creating Equal: My Fight Against Race Preferences* (San Francisco: Encounter Books, 2000).

[9]Stephan Thernstrom, *America in Black and White: One Nation, Indivisible* (New York: Simon & Schuster, 1999).

[10]Connerly, *Creating Equal*; D'Souza, *End of Racism*; P. Shrewsbury, "No Qualifiers Needed: Turning Down the Ironic Insult of Racial Preference," *World* 18 (February 1, 2003).

[11]Of course hate-crime legislation has been advocated not only for racially based crimes but for crimes where the victim's sex, religion or sexual preference is a factor. Since this book is focused on racial issues, I will look at hate crimes only as they deal with race.

[12]Miroslav Volf, *Exclusion and Embrace: A Theological Exploration of Identity, Otherness,*

and Reconciliation (Nashville: Abingdon, 1996).

[13]Rachel F. Moran, *Interracial Intimacy: The Regulation of Race and Romance* (Chicago: University of Chicago Press, 2001).

[14]Douglas S. Massey and Nancy Denton, *American Apartheid: Segregation and the Making of the Underclass* (Cambridge, Mass.: Harvard University Press, 1996).

[15]W. E. B. DuBois, *The Soul of Black Folks* (New York: Dover, 1994); Leslie M. Silko, *Storyteller* (New York: Arcade, 1989); Yoshiko Uchida, *Desert Exile: The Uprooting of a Japanese-American Family* (Seattle: University of Washington Press, 1984); R. Wright, "The Ethics of Living Jim Crow: An Autobiographical Sketch," in *Race, Class and Gender in the United States*, ed. Paula S. Rothenberg (New York: Worth, 2001).

[16]Amy E. Ansell, *New Right, New Racism; Race and Reaction in the United States and Britain* (Washington Square: New York University Press, 1997); Bonilla-Silva, *White Supremacy;* Carr, *Color-Blind Racism;* Richard Delgado and Jean Stefancic, *Critical Race Theory: An Introduction* (New York: New York University Press, 2001); W. M. Wildman and A. D. Davis, "Making Systems of Privilege Visible," in *White Privilege: Essential Readings on the Other Side of Racism*, ed. Paula S. Rothenberg (New York: Worth, 2002), pp. 89-95.

[17]We can understand the overrepresentation of whites by looking at the underrepresentation of racial minorities. For example, in 1994 African Americans made up 1 percent of U.S. Senators, 2 percent of the nation's governors and 5 percent of the U.S. House of Representatives, even though they made up 13 percent of the nation's population. Other racial minority groups are even more underrepresented than African Americans.

[18]John Dovidio, "The Subtlety of Racism," *Training and Development* 47, no. 4 (1993): 51-57.

[19]Federal Glass Ceiling Commission, *Good for Business: Making Full Use of the Nation's Human Capital* (Washington, D.C.: U. S. Government Printing Office, 1995); Dept. of Labor, *Breaking the Glass Ceiling* (Washington, D.C.: U.S. Government Printing Office, 1993).

[20]Contemporary research on modern forms of racism focuses on the majority's desire to maintain an overtly egalitarian stance while supporting public policies that reinforce a racial status quo that serves their interests. See J. B. McConahay, "Modern Racism, Ambivalence, and the Modern Racism Scale," in *Prejudice, Discrimination, and Racism: Theory and Research*, ed. John Dovidio and Samuel L. Gaertner (New York: Academic Press, 1986); Howard Schuman, Charlotte Steeh, Lawrence Bobo and Maria Krysan, *Racial Attitudes in America: Trends and Interpretations* (Cambridge, Mass.: Harvard University Press, 1997); S. Virtanen and L. Huddy, "Old-Fashioned Racism and New Forms of Racial Prejudice," *The Journal of Politics* 60, no. 2 (1998): 311-32.

[21]William J. Bennett, *The Devaluing of America* (Nashville: Thomas Nelson, 1994).

[22]Terry Eastland and William J. Bennett, *Counting by Race: Equality from the Founding Fathers to Bakke and Weber* (New York: Basic Books, 1979).

[23]A great example of the reluctance of white Christians to support the civil rights movement and the effect on blacks fighting for their rights can be seen in King's book *Why We Can't Wait*.

[24]Of course Christians of color who look to legitimize the use of race-based programs through their Christian ideology can also make the same argument.

[25]For a good example of this argument by a black Christian, see A. Bradley, "A New Division, a New Dream," *World* 16, no. 32 (2001): 56.

[26]One critique of whites' tendency to reinterpret King is found in Michael E. Dyson's *I May Not Get There with You: The True Martin Luther King Jr.* (New York: Free Press, 2001). Dyson argues that the tendency of whites to apply a colorblindness emphasis to King's teachings is a misapplication of what King was really saying.

[27]Ralph Reed, *Active Faith: How Christians Are Changing the Soul of American Politics* (New York: Free Press, 1996).

[28]For an example see David Limbaugh, "Race-Based Preferences Harm Society," *WorldNetDaily* (March 30, 2001) <www.worldnetdaily.com/news/article.asp?ARTICLE_ID=22237>.

[29]I do not say this as a critique of such Christians but as a reality that I have experienced. In the introduction to this book, I mention a Bible study about morality that did not discuss racism as a moral issue. I do not believe that the leader was attempting to dismiss racism, but racial issues were not in his frame of reference. Likewise I believe that most white conservative Christians do not mean to dismiss racial issues; but because these issues are not in their common frame of reference, they do not see the moral and spiritual dimensions of racism.

[30]Shrewsbury, "No Qualifiers Needed."

[31]Les Sillars, "Unaffirmative Action: Black Vendor Sues 'Racist' City Program," *World* 14 (1999), p. 23.

[32]David Neff, "Dare We Be Colorblind?" *Christianity Today,* February 3, 1997, pp. 14-15.

Chapter 3: Anglo-Conformity

[1]Daniel Patrick Moynihan, *The Negro Family* (Washington, D.C.: U.S. Department of Labor, 1965).

[2]Stanley Elkins, *Slavery*, 2nd ed. (Chicago: University of Chicago Press, 1968).

[3]S. W. Mintz, "Slavery and Emergent Capitalisms," in *Slavery in the New World,* ed. Laura Foner and Eugene D. Genovese (Englewood Cliffs, N.J.: Prentice-Hall, 1969).

[4]Andrew Billingsley, *Black Families in White America* (Englewood Cliffs, N.J.: Prentice-Hall, 1968); John W. Blassingame, *The Slave Community: Plantation Life in*

the Antebellum South (New York: Oxford University Press, 1972).

[5]I use the word *deviant* in a sociological context. The word describes an action or subcultural tendency which is not normative in the dominant society. The purpose of the word is not to stigmatize contrasting ways of handling social functions but to point out practices that are not accepted by the majority of society.

[6]Oscar Lewis, *Five Families: Mexican Case Studies in the Culture of Poverty* (New York: Basic Books, 1959).

[7]Oscar Lewis, *La Vida: A Puerto Rican Family in the Culture of Poverty—San Juan and New York* (New York: Random House, 1965).

[8]William J. Wilson, *The Declining Significance of Race* (Chicago: University of Chicago Press, 1980).

[9]According to U.S. Census data, in 1999 the median family income for African Americans was 59 percent of the median family income for non-Hispanic whites, and the unemployment rate for blacks was 220 percent of the unemployment rate for whites.

[10]Jennifer L. Hochschild, *Facing Up to the American Dream: Race, Class and the Soul of the Nation* (Princeton, N.J.: Princeton University Press, 1995).

[11]B. Schneider and Y. Lee, "A Model for Academic Success: The School and Home Environment of East Asian Students," *Anthropology and Education Quarterly* 21 (December 1990): 358-77; Thomas Sowell, *Race and Culture: A World View* (New York: Basic Books, 1995).

[12]John J. Miller, *The Unmaking of Americans: How Multiculturalism Has Undermined America's Assimilation Ethic* (New York: Simon & Schuster, 1998); Shelby Steele, *The Content of Our Character: A New Vision of Race in America* (New York: St. Martin's Press, 1990); Stephan Thernstrom, *America in Black and White: One Nation, Indivisible* (New York: Simon & Schuster, 1999).

[13]Research has indicated that economic inequality often leads to resentment from the group that is disadvantaged. See Ernest Gellner, *Nations and Nationalism* (Oxford: Blackwell, 1983); James G. Kellas, *The Politics of Nationalism and Ethnicity* (New York: St. Martin's Press, 1991).

[14]There are those who advocate the removal of capitalism as the way to end racial strife. I disagree; but even if the critics of capitalism are right, they are far from realistic. Capitalism is here to stay for the foreseeable future. Anglo-conformists are correct when they argue that it is better to teach people of color how to deal with capitalism than to hope that the system will disappear.

[15]Leslie G. Carr, *Color-Blind Racism* (Thousand Oaks, Calif.: Sage Publications, 1997); Joe R. Feagin, *Racist America: Roots, Current Realities, and Future Reparations* (New York: Routledge, 2000); Cornel West, *Race Matters* (New York: Vintage Books, 1994).

[16]Nancy Denton and Douglas S. Massey, "Residential Segregation of Blacks, Hispan-

ics, and Asians by Socioeconomic Status and Generation," *Social Science Quarterly* 69 (1988): 797-817; R. Farley, "Residential Segregation in Urbanized Areas in the United States," *Demography* 14 (1977): 497-518.

[17]W. A. V. Clark, "Residential Preferences and Neighborhood Racial Segregation: A Test of the Schelling Segregation Model," *Demography* 28 (1991): 1-19; Robert Lake, *The New Suburbanites: Race and Housing in the Suburbs* (New Brunswick, N.J.: Rutgers University Center for Urban Policy Research, 1981).

[18]Michael Emerson, George Yancey and Karen Chai Kim, "Does Race Matter in Residential Segregation? Exploring the Preferences of White Americans," *American Sociological Review* 66, no. 6 (2001): 922-35; Andrew Hacker, *Two Nations: Black and White, Separate, Hostile, and Unequal* (New York: Ballantine, 1995); Douglas Massey and Nancy Denton, *American Apartheid: Segregation and the Making of the Underclass* (Cambridge, Mass.: Harvard University Press, 1996).

[19]In research that I conducted with Michael Emerson and Karen Chai Kim, we found that whites were not willing to live among blacks even when told that the neighborhood they would be moving into had a low crime rate and good schools. Even having a high-quality neighborhood is not enough motivation for most whites to be willing to live among blacks.

[20]Robert N. Bellah, Richard Madsen, William M. Sullivan, Ann Swindler and Steven M. Tipton, *Habits of the Heart: Individualism and Commitment in American Life* (Berkeley: University of California Press, 1985); Michael O. Emerson and Christian Smith, *Divided by Faith: Evangelical Religion and the Problem of Race in America* (Oxford: Oxford University Press, 2000); J. R. Kluegel, "Trends in Whites' Explanation of the Black-White Gap in Socioeconomic Status, 1977-1989," *American Sociological Review* 55 (1990): 512-25.

[21]William Ryan, *Blaming the Victim* (New York: Random House, 1976).

[22]Sometimes this suggestion is not so subtle as the argument that cultural aspects of racial minorities, such as high divorce rates and large family sizes, have led to economic depression.

[23]Carr, *Color-Blind Racism;* Michael Reich, "The Political-Economic Effects of Racism," in *The Capitalist System: A Radical Analysis of American Society,* ed. Richard C. Edwards, Michael Reich and Thomas E. Weisskopf, 3rd ed. (Englewood Cliffs, N.J.: Prentice-Hall, 1986); A. Szymanski, "Racial Discrimination and White Gain," *American Sociological Review* 41 (1976): 403-14.

[24]One popular neo-Marxian theory is called dual-labor market theory. See E. Bonacich, "A Theory of Ethnic Antagonism: The Split Labor Market," *American Sociological Review* 37 (October 1972): 547-59. This theory contends that barriers between high-wage and low-wage laborers prevent the low-wage laborers from competing with high-wage laborers. The barriers are not based on the abilities of the laborers to do the work; rather they are there to prevent the wealthy from having to compete

with less wealthy, but competent, workers.

[25]Melvin L. Oliver and Thomas M. Shapiro, *Black Wealth/White Wealth: A New Perspective on Racial Inequality* (New York: Routledge, 1995), pp. 160-69.

[26]In John 14:6, Jesus claims to be *the way* to God. Jesus claims a unity with God which is unmatched by any other being. He claims that we can find ultimate truth only in recognition of him. Jesus' claim assumes that there is a truth out there to be found. Some secular ideologies see Christianity as a path for some but not for others. They are based on modernist philosophy, which says that each person has the ability to create his or her own understanding of the truth. Supporters of orthodox or traditional theologies have rejected the modernist twist to Christian understanding, although the degree to which Christians adhere to modernism varies greatly.

[27]In a recent reference book by James Dobson, the only place racial issues are brought up is an admonishment against the cultural relativism found in multiculturalism (James Dobson, *The Complete Marriage and Family Home Reference Guide* [Carol Stream, Ill.: Tyndale House, 2000]). To be fair, Dobson was not attempting to articulate any sort of racial philosophy, but he used a right-wrong dichotomy to criticize a commonly accepted way of dealing with racial issues. It is not a stretch of logic to believe that a significant number of Christians also use the right-wrong dichotomy to assert the worth of certain cultural values over those of other cultures.

[28]Much of the advice given in Proverbs not only has a moral dimension but also holds out the promise of economic benefits.

[29]See Star Parker, *Pimps, Whores and Welfare Brats: From Welfare Cheat to Conservative Messenger* (New York: Pocket Books, 1998).

[30]Ibid., p. 107.

[31]R. Frame, "Helping the Poor Help Themselves," *Christianity Today*, February 3, 1997, pp. 70-73; B. Jones IV, "Mrs. Taylor's Neighborhood," *World*, May 16, 1998, p. 13; L. Vincent, "Watts, Rising," *World*, June 9, 2001, pp. 22-25; D. Zhan, R. Eric and M. Norwich, "Churches in Action," *Leadership Journal* (Spring 2003).

[32]Situation ethics is a theological idea championed most notably by Joseph Fletcher in *Situation Ethics: The New Morality* (Louisville, Ky.: Westminster John Knox Press, 1997). The concept is that as long as we can justify our actions with love, then any actions we take are appropriate. Of course this philosophy fails because humans can interpret their own actions as loving even when those actions are to meet a selfish goal. The philosophy of situation ethics allows people of color to ignore their own responsibilities and blame majority group members for their problems. Anglo-conformity can offset situation ethics by calling on both whites and people of color to seek out a right path to morality.

[33]We should not make the seemingly logical leap that all those in poverty are there

because of their sins. Many of the disciples died in poverty, and today many Christians are poor through no fault of their own. Christians may find themselves called to positions in society that are not economically beneficial. Rather than a simplistic correlation of righteousness to wealth, we should realize that our Lord will provide us with enough wealth to fulfill the purpose to which he has called us. Our sins may keep us from that level of wealth and thus lead us to spiritual frustration. In this case our lack of material resources is not a punishment in and of itself, but it is a punishment in that it prevents us from fully living out what God has intended for us.

[34]For example, many cultures rely on extended families instead of the nuclear families more typical to European American Christians. Majority group Christians may criticize adult children who choose to live with their parents rather than strike out on their own. Such criticism is not biblical, since there is no scriptural support for an emphasis on nuclear families. There is a significant need for Christians to distinguish between issues that are cultural, and thus optional, and those that are scriptural, and thus mandatory for a healthy Christian walk.

[35]For example, Wilson points out the effects of historic racism on the lives of African Americans, even as he argues that contemporary racism is not the true source of racial disparity today (Wilson, *Declining Significance of Race*).

Chapter 4: Multiculturalism

[1]E. Hu-DeHart, "Rethinking America: The Practice of Politics of Multiculturalism in Higher Education," in *Beyond a Dream Deferred: Multicultural Education and the Politics of Excellence,* ed. Becky W. Thompson and Sangeeta Tyagi (Minneapolis: University of Minnesota Press, 1993); Kent L. Koppelman and R. Lee Goodhart, *Understanding Human Differences: Multicultural Education for a Diverse America* (Boston: Pearson Education, 2005); Ronald Takaki, *A Different Mirror: A History of Multicultural America* (Boston: Little, Brown, 1994); C. James Trotman, introduction to *Multiculturalism: Roots and Realities,* ed. C. James Trotman (Bloomington: Indiana University Press, 2002), pp. ix-xvii; T. Turner, "Anthropology and Multiculturalism: What Is Anthropology That Multiculturalists Should Be Mindful of It?" in *Multiculturalism: A Critical Reader,* ed. David T. Goldberg (Oxford: Blackwell, 1994), pp. 406-25.

[2]A. T. Kisubi, "Ideological Perspectives on Multiculturalism," in *Multiculturalism in a Cross-National Perspective,* ed. Michael Burayidi (Lanham, Md.: University Press of America, 1997), pp. 15-35; Koppelman and Goodhart, *Understanding Human Differences;* C. W. Watson, *Multiculturalism* (Philadelphia: Open University Press, 2000).

[3]M. Pachen, *Diversity and Unity: Relations Between Racial Ethnic Groups* (Chicago: Nelson-Hall Publishers, 1999), p. 275.

[4]Lisa D. Delpit, *Other People's Children: Cultural Conflict in the Classroom* (New York: New Press, 1996); A. G. Hilliard, "Conceptual Confusion and the Persistence of Group Oppression Through Education," *Equity and Excellence* 24, no. 1 (1988): 36-43; Gary R. Howard, *We Can't Teach What We Don't Know: White Teachers, Multiracial Schools* (New York: Teacher College Press, 1999); Koppelman and Goodhart, *Understanding Human Differences;* Sonia Nieto, *Affirming Diversity: The Sociopolitical Context of Multicultural Education,* 3rd ed. (Boston: Allyn and Bacon, 1999); Christine Sleeter and Carl Grant, *Making Choices for Multicultural Education,* 3rd ed. (New York: Merrill, 1999).

[5]Taylor Cox, *Creating the Multicultural Organization: A Strategy for Capturing the Power of Diversity* (San Francisco: Jossey-Bass, 2001); Sherron B. Kenton and Deborah Valentine, *Crosstalk: Communicating in a Multicultural Workplace* (Upper Saddle River, N.J.: Prentice-Hall, 1996); J. L. Nicklin, "Helping to Manage Diversity in the Workforce," *Chronicle of Higher Education,* September 30, 1992, p. A5; Norma Carr-Rufino, *Managing Diversity: People Skills for a Multicultural Workplace* (Boston: Pearson Custom Publishing, 2002).

[6]Elaine P. Congress, ed., *Multicultural Perspectives in Working with Families* (New York: Springer Publication Company, 1997); Jonathan H. S. Fuller and P. D. Toon, *Medical Practice in a Multicultural Society* (Woburn, Mass · Butterworth Heinemann Medical, 1988); Warwick Tie, *Legal Pluralism: Toward a Multicultural Conception of Law* (Brookfield, Vt.: Dartmouth Publishing, 1999); Nicholas Vacc, Susan Devaney, and Joe Wittmer, *Experiencing and Counseling Multicultural and Diverse Populations* (Bristol, Penn.: Accelerated Development, 1995).

[7]James Bank, *Teaching Strategies for Ethnic Studies* (Boston: Allyn and Bacon, 1987); W. A. Henry, "Beyond the Melting Pot," *Time,* April 9, 1990, pp. 28-31; Koppelman and Goodhart, *Understanding Human Differences;* Takaki, *A Different Mirror;* C. Taylor, "The Politics of Recognition," in *Multiculturalism: A Critical Reader,* ed. David T. Goldberg (Malden, Mass.: Blackwell, 1994), pp. 75-106.

[8]S. Dale McLemore, Harriet D. Romo and Susan G. Baker, *Racial and Ethnic Relations in America* (Boston: Allyn and Bacon, 2001), p. 30; S. J. Whitfield, "America's Melting Pot Ideal and Horace Kallen," *Society* 36, no. 6 (1999): 53-55.

[9]In many ways the United States has fallen short of this ideal. Canada has more thoroughly incorporated the concepts of multiculturalism. For example, in Canada the government financially supports ethnic associations, schools and organizations that help maintain the distinct cultures within their borders. In Canada the public sector rather than the private market sponsors multiculturalism.

[10]McLemore, Romo and Baker, *Racial and Ethnic Relations,* p. 581.

[11]P. McLaren, "White Terror and Oppositional Agency: Towards a Critical Multiculturalism," in *Multiculturalism: A Critical Reader,* ed. David T. Goldberg (Malden, Mass.: Blackwell, 1994), pp. 45-74; M. E. Spencer, "Multiculturalism, Political

Correctness and the Politics of Identity," *Sociological Forum* 9 (December 1994): 547-67.

[12]Nathan Glazer, *We Are All Multiculturalists Now* (Cambridge, Mass.: Harvard University Press, 1998).

[13]Abraham F. Citron, *The Rightness of Whiteness: The World of the White Child in a Segregated Society* (Detroit: Michigan-Ohio Regional Educational Laboratory, 1969); Hu-DeHart, "Rethinking America"; M. Manning, "Racism and Multicultural Democracy," in *Double Exposure: Poverty and Race in America,* ed. C. Hartman (Armonk, N.Y.: M. E. Sharp, 1997), pp. 151-60; McLaren, "White Terror"; J. Schiele, "Afrocentricity: Implications for Higher Education," *Journal of Black Studies* 25, no. 2 (1994): 150-69.

[14]Stokely Carmichael and Charles V. Hamilton, *Black Power: The Politics of Liberation in America* (New York: Vintage, 1967); Richard Delgado and Jean Stefancic, *Critical Race Theory: An Introduction* (New York: New York University Press, 2001); J. K. Donner, "Learning from Black Folks," in *Critical Race Theory Perspectives on Social Studies: The Profession, Policies, and Curriculum,* ed. G. Ladson-Billing (Greenwich, Conn.: Information Age Publishing, 2003); Hu-DeHart, "Rethinking America"; G. Ladson-Billing, "Lies My Teacher Still Tells," in *Critical Race Theory Perspectives,* ed. G. Ladson-Billing; William Newman, *American Pluralism* (New York: Harper & Row, 1973).

[15]A. Athanases, D. Christiano and E. Lay, "Fostering Empathy and Finding Common Ground in Multiethnic Classes," *English Journal* 84 (1995): 26-34; Hans Bak, "The Health is On: Canon or Kaleidoscope," in *Multiculturalism and the Canon of American Culture,* ed. Hans Bak (Amsterdam: VU University Press, 1993), pp. 65-80; Henry, "Beyond the Melting Pot"; Sleeter and Grant, *Making Choices.*

[16]Bellah et al., *Habits of the Heart;* Eduardo Bonilla-Silva and Amanda Lewis, "The 'New Racism': Toward an Analysis of the U.S. Racial Structure, 1960s-1990s," in *Race, Ethnicity and Nationality in the United States: Toward the Twenty-First Century,* ed. Paul Wong (Boulder, Colo.: Westview Press, 1998), pp. 55-101; Kluegel, "Trends in Whites' Explanation."

[17]C. I. Cohen, K. Hyland and C. Magai, "Depression Among African American Nursing Home Patients with Dementia," *American Journal of Psychiatry* 6 (1998): 162-75; J. E. Turnbull and A. Mui, "Mental Health Status and Needs of Black and White Elderly: Differences in Depression," in *Handbook on Ethnicity, Aging, and Mental Health,* ed. Deborah K. Padgett (Westport, Conn.: Greenwood Press, 1995), pp. 73-98.

[18]For examples of such criticism, see P. McLaren, "White Terror and Oppositional Agency," pp. 45-74; Koppelman and Goodhart, *Understanding Human Differences.*

[19]Some may claim that certain cultures *are* better than others. Who would not prefer the relatively peaceful Nez Perces to the society of Nazi Germany? But if multiculturalists can claim that entire races of peoples have superior cultures, then they run

into the same trap they are trying to help society escape. If we argue that Native American culture is superior to European American culture, then we have provided justification for the suppression of European American culture. Ironically the logical conclusion for multiculturalists who argue that some cultures are better than others is the reduction of the cultures that we support in our society, not celebration of the cultures that already exist.

[20]Oscar Lewis, *La Vida: A Puerto Rican Family in the Culture of Poverty—San Juan and New York* (New York: Random House, 1965); Daniel Patrick Moynihan, *The Negro Family* (Washington, D.C.: U.S. Department of Labor; 1965); David Popenoe, *Disturbing the Nest: Family Change and Decline in Modern Societies* (New York: Aldine de Gruyter, 1988).

[21]Laurence Steinberg, *Beyond the Classroom* (New York: Simon and Schuster, 1997).

[22]Elizabeth H. Boyle, *Female Genital Cutting: Cultural Conflict in the Global Community* (Baltimore: Johns Hopkins University Press, 2002); Anika Rahman and Nahid Toubia, *Female Genital Mutilation: A Practical Guide to Worldwide Laws and Policies*, vol. 3 (London: Zed Books, 2000).

[23]Stan D. Gaede, *When Tolerance Is No Virtue: Political Correctness, Multiculturalism and the Future of Truth and Justice* (Downers Grove, Ill.: InterVarsity Press, 1993).

[24]A few years ago I saw a television show that was a morbid version of *Candid Camera*. An unsuspecting woman was set up to be a maid for a modern couple who pretended to practice cannibalism. When the couple asked her to join them in eating human flesh, she responded in a typical multicultural fashion, something like, "That is all right for you if that is what you want to do, but I do not choose to eat other people." I do not mean to say that multiculturalists support eating people. My point is that the woman's answer was completely consistent with the multiculturalist model. Although she found the practice of cannibalism repulsive, and so would most of the human race, she refrained from passing judgment on it. If we take the philosophy of multiculturalism seriously, it is difficult to fault the woman's answer.

[25]Curtiss Paul DeYoung, *Coming Together: The Bible's Message in an Age of Diversity* (Valley Forge, Penn.: Judson Press, 1995); Glen Usry and Craig S. Keener, *Black Man's Religion: Can Christianity Be Afrocentric?* (Downers Grove, Ill.: InterVarsity Press, 1996).

[26]Elizabeth Conde-Frazier, S. Steve Kang and Gary A. Parrett, *A Many Colored Kingdom: Multicultural Dynamics for Spiritual Formation* (Grand Rapids: Baker, 2004); J. J. Han, "The Uses of Reading Ethnic Minority Literature: The Christian Multiculturalism" (paper presented at the National Faculty Leadership Conference, Chicago, 2001).

[27]Y. Delk, "A Time for Action: Building Strategy to Dismantle Racism," *Sojourners* 27 (1998): 25; V. Elizondo, "Benevolent Tolerance or Humble Reverence? A Vision for

Multicultural Religious Education," in *Multicultural Religious Education*, ed. Barbara Wilkerson (Birmingham, Ala.: Religious Education Press, 1997), pp. 395-405; Randy Woodley, *Living in Color: Embracing God's Passion for Diversity* (Downers Grove, Ill.: InterVarsity Press, 2004).

[28]Paul-Gordon Chandler, *God's Global Mosaic: What We Can Learn from Christians Around the World* (Downers Grove, Ill: InterVarsity Press, 2000); Conde-Frazier et al., *Many Colored Kingdom*; A. Harman, "Racism in Australia," *Theological Forum* 25 (1997): 4; Woodley, *Living in Color*.

[29]Randy Woodley, *Mixed Blood Not Mixed Up: Finding God-Given Identity in a Multicultural World* (Hayden, Ala.: Eagle's Wings Ministry, 2000); Woodley, *Living in Color*.

[30]Clarence Shuler, *Winning the Race to Unity: Is Racial Reconciliation Really Working?* (Chicago: Moody Press, 2003).

Chapter 5: White Responsibility

[1]Lawrence Bobo, J. R. Kluegel and R. A. Smith, "Laissez-Faire Racism: The Crystallization of a Kinder, Gentler, Antiblack Ideology," in *Racial Attitudes in the 1990s: Continuity and Change*, ed. Steven A. Tuch and Jack K. Martin (Westport, Conn.: Praeger, 1997), pp. 15-42; Lawrence Bobo and R. A. Smith, "From Jim Crow Racism to Laissez-Faire Racism: The Transformation of Racial Attitudes," in *Beyond Pluralism: The Conception of Groups and Group Identities in America*, ed. Wendy F. Katkin, Ned Landsman and Andrea Tyree (Urbana: University of Illinois Press, 1998).

[2]Leslie Carr, *Color-Blind Racism* (Thousand Oaks, Calif.: Sage, 1997); C. Daniels, "Black Racist: The Debate Continues," *Community Contact* 7, no. 10 (1998): 4; J. Weisberg, "Thin Skins," *New Republic*, February 18, 1991, p. 23.

[3]I have conducted research which indicates that individuals of color are no more likely than majority group members to agree that racial minorities cannot be racist (George Yancey, " 'Blacks Cannot Be Racists': A Look at How European-Americans, African-Americans, Hispanic-Americans, and Asian-Americans Perceive Minority Racism," *Michigan Sociological Review* 19 [2005]). It seems that the leaders within minority communities, not the common folks, are the ones who maintain that only whites can be racists.

[4]Many of these ideas have been around longer than the emergence of the modern civil rights movement. For example, in *The Soul of Black Folks* (New York: Dover Publications, 1994), W. E. B. DuBois developed early ideas of the struggle of African Americans as they encounter the racist system in the United States.

[5]Richard Delgado and Jean Stefancic, *Critical Race Theory: An Introduction* (New York: New York University Press, 2001).

[6]Monica Moorehead, "Reparations and Black Liberation," *Workers World Newspaper* 40, no. 22 (June 6, 2002): 1, 7; Randall Robinson, *The Debt: What America Owes to*

Blacks (New York: Penguin Putman, 2000); R. Westley, "Many Billions Gone: Is It Time to Reconsider the Case for Black Reparations?" in *Should America Pay? Slavery and the Raging Debate on Reparations,* ed. Raymond A. Winbush (New York: Amistad, 2003).

[7]Most notably some have argued that the Native Americans and African Americans were promised resources in exchange for their land and labor. While Native Americans have been at least partially repaid for their land through contemporary treaty rights, the little they have gained cannot make up for what has been taken from them. Furthermore, there is no argument that African Americans have yet received even part of the "forty acres and a mule" that they were promised.

[8]George Yancey, *Beyond Black and White: Reflections on Racial Reconciliation* (Grand Rapids: Baker, 1996).

[9]Peggy McIntosh, "White Privilege: Unpacking the Invisible Knapsack," in *White Privilege: Essential Readings on the Other Side of Racism,* ed. Paula S. Rothenberg (New York: Worth, 2002), pp. 97-102.

[10]An excellent book on white privilege is Paula S. Rothenberg, ed., *White Privilege: Essential Readings on the Other Side of Racism.*

[11]Donald R. Kinder and Lynn M. Sanders, *Divided by Color: Racial Politics and Democratic Ideals* (Chicago: University of Chicago Press, 1996); Howard Schuman et al., *Racial Attitudes in America: Trends and Interpretations* (Cambridge, Mass.: Harvard University Press, 1997).

[12]Julia A. Boyd, *In the Company of My Sisters: Black Women and Self-Esteem* (New York: Plume Books, 1997); Jawanza Kunjufu, *Countering the Conspiracy to Destroy Black Boys* (Chicago: African American Images, 1990); Alexander Thomas and Samuel Sillen, *Racism and Psychiatry* (New York: Bruner-Mazel, 1972); D. Wilkinson, "Minority Women: Social-Cultural Issues," in *Women and Psychotherapy,* ed. Annette M. Brodsky and Rachel T. Hare-Mustin (New York: Guilford, 1980), pp. 295-97.

[13]This argument is made in Robert N. Bellah et al., *Habits of the Heart: Individualism and Commitment in American Life* (Berkeley: University of California Press, 1985), pp. 20-22. Furthermore, Michael Emerson and Christian Smith in *Divided by Faith* (Oxford: Oxford University Press, 2000) demonstrate that white Christians have higher levels of freewill individualism than other whites (p. 76).

[14]To say that a society is *racialized* means that individuals' racial identity heavily shapes their lives. Bonilla-Silva discusses how oppressive social systems based on race impact our lives (Eduardo Bonilla-Silva, "Rethinking Racism: Towards a Structural Interpretation," *American Sociological Review* 62 [1997]: 465-80).

[15]Eduardo Bonilla-Silva, *White Supremacy and Racism in the Post-Civil Rights Era* (Boulder, Colo.: Lynne Reinner Publishers, 2001); Emerson and Smith, *Divided by Faith.*

[16]For example, Andrew Hacker, *Two Nations: Black and White, Separate, Hostile and Unequal* (New York: Ballantine, 1995); Joe R. Feagin, *Racist America: Roots, Current Re-*

alities, and Future Reparations (New York: Routledge, 2000); and McIntosh, "White Privilege" reflect white secular viewpoints. Joseph Barndt, *Dismantling Racism: The Continuing Challenge to White America* (Minneapolis: Augsburg Fortress, 1991) is an example of a white Christian adherent of the white responsibility model.

[17]To "play the race card" is to make a charge of racism even when there is no evidence that racism exists. I will discuss this concept further in chapter 8.

[18]The origin of our sin is a question hotly debated by theologians and philosophers. For example, Tennant contends that sin is a part our human nature (Frederick F. Tennant, *The Origin and Propagation of Sin* [Cambridge: Cambridge University Press, 1902]). As we have developed an evolutionary sense of morality, we have become aware of our human failings. On the other hand, Niebuhr sees sin as a result of our realization of our own limits as humans (Reinhold Niebuhr, *The Nature and Destiny of Man* [New York: Scribner's Sons, 1941]). The insecurity that we feel because of our own shortcomings leads us to accept the concept of human sin. A more traditional interpretation is that sin is the spiritual inheritance of Adam, passed down to all of us regardless of our personal awareness of it or our insecurities. Of course there are other attempts to explain sin, such as liberation theology (Justo González and Catherine González, *Liberation Preaching: The Pulpit and the Oppressed* [Nashville: Abingdon, 1980]; Gustavo Gutiérrez, *A Theology of Liberation: History, Politics and Salvation* [Maryknoll, N.Y.: Orbis, 1973]) or human competition (H. S. Elliott, *Can Religious Education Be Christian?* [New York: Macmillan, 1940]). Much of Christianity aims to help us understand our sinful nature and personal shortcomings while providing a theological way for us to come to terms with our human depravity. This argument is the basis of my claim that dealing with our sin nature is at the core of how Christians understand their faith.

[19]Perhaps the best-known popular treatment of structural sin is Ron Sider's *Rich Christians in an Age of Hunger: A Biblical Study* (Downers Grove, Ill.: InterVarsity Press, 1978).

[20]One example is the recent statement from the Illinois Conference of the United Church of Christ, *Resolution Regarding Reparations for Slavery,* June 2002.

[21]James Cone, *Black Theology and Black Power* (New York: Seabury, 1969).

[22]The major initiator of liberation theology is Gustavo Gutiérrez (*A Theology of Liberation*). Other proponents include Phillip Berryman, *Liberation Theology* (New York: Pantheon, 1987); Justo González and Catherine González, *Liberation Preaching;* and Leonardo Boff and Clodovis Boff, *Introducing Liberation Theology* (Maryknoll, N.Y.: Orbis, 1987).

Chapter 6: Toward Constructing a Christian Solution to the Problem of Racism
[1]This is argued by Robert S. McGee in *The Search for Significance: Seeing Your True Worth Through God's Eyes* (Nashville: W Publishing, 1998).

[2]Some Christians may not accept the premise that we have a sin nature. They prefer to believe that human perfectibility is possible. Of course people who call themselves Christians endorse all sorts of philosophies. But at some point, if our Christianity means anything, we have to set boundaries on what it means to be a Christian. So although I want to present a broad and inclusive Christian faith, I have to consider some limits on what it means to be a Christian. I believe that the absence of a sin nature would nullify Christ's need to give his life for us. I question whether an ideology which denies the sin nature can be called Christian. We may differ on how the sin nature manifests itself; but if we do not acknowledge our fallen nature, how can we accept the healing that Christ offers us?

[3]I do not pretend to be an expert on alternative religions, but I teach a Sociology of Religion class on a regular basis. I have not yet encountered a non-Christian religion that conceptualizes the human sin nature in quite the same way as Christianity. My understanding of Eastern religions is that sin is either nonexistent (Buddhism) or merely the opposite of good (Taoism). In Western non-Christian religions (such as Islam) sin is something to be defeated by the actions of humans; adherents seek to perfectly obey their deity rather than repent of their sin. The idea that sin is a part of who we are, not merely something we do, is missing from non-Christian religions. If my observations are correct, Christians have spiritual insight into racial problems that is missing in other systems of faith.

[4]Miroslav Volf correctly points out that in times of intergroup conflict, Christians tend to become overcommitted to their culture (Volf, *Exclusion and Embrace* [Nashville: Abingdon, 1996]). Christians then become allies for those of their own racial group, regardless of the fairness of the group's position. Given the racial strife in our society, we would do well to heed Volf's warning.

[5]Robert Pyne observes that even when we try to maintain good motivations, sin has a way of twisting those motivations into selfishness (Pyne, *Humanity and Sin: The Creation, Fall and Redemption of Humanity* [Nashville: Word, 1999]). The power of sin is so corrupting and pervasive that it affects our actions even when we believe we are doing the right thing.

[6]Cornelius Plantinga Jr., *Not the Way It's Supposed to Be* (Grand Rapids: Eerdmans, 1995).

[7]Millard Erickson points out that those who believe humanity is basically good want to fix social structures, while those who believe humanity is basically corrupt want to fix people (Erickson, *Christian Theology*, 2nd ed. [Grand Rapids: Baker, 1998]). Based on such an analysis, Christian supporters of colorblindness and Anglo-conformity hold to the individualistic definition of sin, while Christian supporters of multiculturalism and white responsibility hold to the structural definition.

[8]Theologians dispute the doctrine of original sin, but even those who deny the con-

cept do not argue that any of us is perfect. One way or another, sin eventually enters and dominates our lives.

[9]Charles Colson tells a great story to illustrate this point (Charles Colson, *Loving God* [Grand Rapids: Zondervan, 1997], pp. 101-2). He tells of a time when he was a military officer and caught a food peddler on a U.S. military base located in a foreign country. He knew that technically the man was in the wrong, but that he was just trying to make a living. He could have just removed the man from the base. However, he confiscated the peddler's food to give to his soldiers and to win the soldier's approval. Colson related that he did this not because it was right but because he had the power to do it. He wanted to sin, and because he had the power to get away with his sins, he engaged in this type of thievery. Colson uses this story to show that sin is not just an occasional accident but is hardwired into our being. Only the power of a loving God can end our slavery to the sin within us.

[10]Colson, *Loving God,* p. 102.

[11]Erickson discusses how sin is often our attempt to meet legitimate needs by methods that transgress the proper boundaries (Erickson, *Christian Theology,* pp. 614-15). For example, our desire for money and the material goods we need to keep us alive is normal and not sinful. When we pervert that desire into hoarding and greed, we cross the line into sin. In racial matters, there is nothing wrong with looking out for our group to make sure our own people are taken care of. Sin arises when our desire becomes so ethnocentric that we begin to exploit and take advantage of other groups.

[12]One tool that Satan uses against us is to deny the truth of the spiritual dimension of life. C. S. Lewis argued this dramatically in *The Screwtape Letters* (New York: Macmillan, 1976). If worldly forces are able to keep us focused only on nonsupernatural answers, then they rob us of the Lord's resources to battle racism. For this reason I believe that Christians must add a spiritual dynamic to the definition of racism and their plans to battle it. Brenda Salter-McNeil and Rick Richardson have written an excellent book that deals with the spiritual and practical aspects of racism (Salter-McNeil and Richardson, *The Heart of Racial Justice: How Soul Change Leads to Social Change* [Downers Grove, Ill.: InterVarsity Press, 2005]).

[13]For example, I notice that many people who talk about tolerance exhibit their own brand of intolerance when they talk about those who disagree with them politically or religiously. Then they use terms such as *right wing* and *fundamentalist* in a disparaging and dehumanizing manner. We may label such progressives as hypocrites, but the accusation misses the point. All of us set standards that we fail to meet. Our sin nature encourages us to ignore our own hypocrisy while we draw attention to the hypocrisy of our opponents.

[14]Leon Morris argues that Paul talks of sin as a power that holds us in bondage (Morris, *New Testament Theology* [Grand Rapids: Zondervan, 1990]). Just as a slave is

sold to a master whether the slave likes it or not, we come under the power of sin whether we like it or not. We may make a Herculean attempt to avoid a particular sin, but eventually the fact that we are sinners will overwhelm us, and we will give in to our own selfishness and greed. Such is the situation for the unregenerate. We cannot hope to find ultimate solutions to the sinful state of racism without also ending the slavery of sin in our lives.

[15]For a contemporary example of the horrors that people of color can do, we only need to look at Sudan and the enslavement practiced by the black Sudanese. The ability to oppress people of other races is not limited to Europeans or European Americans. It is found in those of all races.

[16]Of the major world religions, only the Christian faith attempts to deal with the fallen state of humans by sending a deity to bring them salvation. The salvation Christ offers is the core element of Christianity. Pyne points out that salvation is generally connected to a renewal of creation, and thus can be seen as the way to overcome our human depravity (*Humanity and Sin,* pp. 60-61).

Another way to look at salvation is with its Hebraic definition: salvation is wholeness, and our sin nature makes us less than fully human. Salvation is seen as completing us and making us fully human. Applied to racism, it means that a racialized society is a less than whole society until we bring true salvation.

Clearly, how *salvation* is defined differs in different theologies. A more orthodox theology focuses on salvation as the way for an individual to reach the person of God. Liberation theology conceptualizes salvation as freedom from the economic oppression of capitalism. Existential theology calls humans to find their true self amidst the illusions of society. Likewise the way salvation helps us to overcome our human depravity differs in different theologies. Orthodox theology perceives salvation as the reconnection of a spiritual relationship with God. Liberation theology envisions the development of socialism in place of capitalism. Existential theology paints a picture of individuals achieving self-actualization. Despite the different definitions of salvation, the pursuit of salvation remains a key element of the Christian faith.

[17]Plantinga, *Not the Way It's Supposed to Be.*

[18]Volf points out that striving after reconciliation, even if we know that reconciliation will not be complete, creates lasting alterations in our identities. In other words, even if we do not achieve our ultimate goals, we will create more intergroup harmony through our efforts (Volf, *Exclusion and Embrace,* pp. 109-10).

[19]This is based on a premillennial or amillennial view of the last days. Either stance states that we will not see the paradise promised us in the Scriptures until the second coming of Christ. Those who hold a postmillennial view believe that the world will be converted and heaven will begin on earth due to the spread of the gospel everywhere. Support for the postmillennial view has declined in recent times

(Erickson, *Christian Theology*), perhaps because people realize how much things would have to change in order for paradise to come, and because there is apparently no strong biblical grounds for earthly rule by Christ. I feel some comfort in dismissing the postmillennial view in my analysis, although its supporters will undoubtedly disagree.

[20]Mark McMinn, *Why Sin Matters: The Surprising Relationship Between Our Sin and God's Grace* (Wheaton, Ill.: Tyndale House, 2004).

[21]As Plantinga writes, "Sin is remarkably generative: sin yields more and more sin" (Plantinga, *Not the Way It's Supposed to Be*, p. 53). The sinful actions of the perpetrator can lead to a sinful and vengeful response from the victim. The perpetrator, understanding the potential of such a response, then becomes more unwilling to admit wrongdoing, allowing the first sin to produce even more wrong.

[22]This is especially problematic because in several places in the Scriptures we are admonished to confess our sins to each other (Matthew 5:23-24; Luke 17:3-4; James 5:16). If we are going to overcome the sins of racism, then confession from one human to another appears to be a critical element. Our tendency to hide our sin nature makes such confessions difficult if not impossible.

[23]As we can see in Luke 19:8, there are times when we have to pay back those we have victimized by our sins.

[24]This is a problem because Jesus tells us to forgive as part of seeking forgiveness (Matthew 6:12). God gave up his right to demand what we owe him, yet it is difficult for us to do the same for other people. Perhaps Jesus means for us to know just how difficult forgiveness is when he requires us to forgive others as an aspect of receiving forgiveness from God. We will be unlikely to take his forgiveness for granted when we have undergone the struggle to forgive someone who has wronged us.

[25]George Yancey, *Beyond Black and White: Reflections on Racial Reconciliation* (Grand Rapids: Baker, 1996), pp. 125-30.

Chapter 7: Sin Nature and European Americans

[1]Not all people of color view racial issues as structural. I have documented that African Americans tend to have more structuralist racial attitudes than Hispanic and Asian Americans (Yancey, *Who Is White? Latinos, Asians, and the New Black/Nonblack Divide* [Boulder, Colo.: Lynne Rienner Publishers, 2003]). Yet nonblack racial minorities were still less individualistic than majority group members.

[2]There are disturbing similarities between the treatment of Japanese Americans during World War II and the treatment of Middle Easterners today during our war on terror. It is too simplistic to argue that the situations are exactly the same, but the similarities are close enough to make me uncomfortable.

[3]*Owned* may be an incorrect term since not all Native Americans had a concept of

land ownership. Some tribes did not mind if others used their land as long as they were not using it at the time, a concept distinct from our modern idea of exclusive land ownership. Nevertheless, Native Americans had a claim to all the lands in the Americas before the arrival of the Europeans.

[4]For more detailed information about some of the horrible ways Natives were treated, see Dee Brown, *Bury My Heart at Wounded Knee: An Indian History of the American West* (New York: Holt, Rinehart and Winston, 1971).

[5]Of course as an African American I am in a unique position. On the one hand, I have bought a house and thus have indirectly benefited from the oppression of Native Americans. On the other hand, in our history there have been times that Native Americans were able to abuse African Americans and vice versa. These situations complicate the argument about historic oppression, but they do not eliminate its basic premise: that sins against certain racial groups have helped other racial groups prosper.

[6]A study by Gunnar Myrdal indicated that whites feared interpersonal relations with blacks, such as friendships and marriages, more than they feared equal access to jobs and other economic resources. Ironically, Myrdal also found that blacks desired economic resources more than interpersonal relationships (Myrdal, *An American Dilemma: The Negro Problem and Modern Democracy* [New York: McGraw-Hill, 1964]).

[7]Segregation happens even when people do not realize it. For example, when I taught in Wisconsin I lived about forty miles from Madison, a city of about 200,000 and about 2 percent black. One of my colleagues, a rather progressive political science teacher, lived in Madison and told me there was no racial segregation there. My wife, Sherelyn, found the black area of town on her second visit and even started to shop at some of the stores there. My colleague had fooled herself into thinking that Madison was more racially progressive than it was. I wonder how many more white residents of Madison are also ignorant of the black underclass that is a part of their city.

[8]According to Andrew Hacker, once a neighborhood becomes 8 percent black, a process begins which inevitably leads to the creation of an all-black community (Hacker, *Two Nations: Black and White, Separate, Hostile and Unequal* [New York: Ballantine, 1995], p. 41).

[9]Douglas Massey and Nancy Denton, *American Apartheid: Segregation and the Making of the Underclass* (Cambridge, Mass.: Harvard University Press, 1996), chaps. 4-5. If you desire a more complete explanation of why residential segregation is so injurious to African Americans, I highly recommend their book.

[10]For example, if each home in a school district must provide an average of $1,000 to adequately fund the schools, then you must tax a home worth $50,000 at a 2 percent tax rate, while a home worth $100,000 can be taxed at a 1 percent rate.

[11]Valiant attempts have been made to change this situation. Texas has implemented a type of Robin Hood system, whereby richer school districts provide a source of income for poorer ones. The system has been under attack, and I am unsure whether it will still be in place by the time this book is published. It is no surprise that critics of the plan tend to live in or represent the wealthier districts.

[12]Elijah Anderson, *Streetwise: Race, Class and Change in an Urban Community* (Chicago: University of Chicago Press, 1990); Kenneth B. Clark, *Dark Ghetto: Dilemmas of Social Power* (New York: Harper, 1965); Massey and Denton, *American Apartheid.*

[13]Claud Anderson, *Black Labor, White Wealth: The Search for Power and Economic Justice* (Bethesda, Md.: Powernomics Corporation in America, 1994); Melvin L. Oliver and Thomas M. Shapiro, *Black Wealth/White Wealth: A New Perspective on Racial Inequality* (New York: Routledge, 1995).

[14]David Cole, *No Equal Justice: Race and Class in the American Criminal Justice System* (New York: New Press, 2000); Marvin A. Free, *African Americans and the Criminal Justice System* (New York: Garland, 1995); Samuel Walker, Cassia Spohn and Miriam Delone, *The Color of Justice: Race, Ethnicity and Crime in America* (Belmont, Calif.: Wadsworth, 1999).

[15]Millard J. Erickson, *Christian Theology,* 2nd ed. (Grand Rapids: Baker, 1998); Leon Morris, *New Testament Theology* (Grand Rapids: Zondervan, 1990).

[16]Michael Cassidy, *The Passing Summer* (Ventura, Calif.: Regal Books, 1989); William E. Pannell, *The Coming Race Wars? A Cry for Reconciliation* (Grand Rapids: Zondervan, 1993); Spencer Perkins and Chris Rice, *More Than Equals: Racial Healing for the Sake of the Gospel* (Downers Grove, Ill.: InterVarsity Press, 2000); Raleigh Washington and Glen Kehrein, *Breaking Down Walls: A Model for Reconciliation in an Age of Strife* (Chicago: Moody Press, 1993).

[17]James 1:23-24 tells us that we cannot merely hear the word of God but must also act on it. Likewise whites cannot merely admit there is institutional sin but must seek to become allies with people of color in an effort to end that sin.

[18]Eduardo Bonilla-Silva, *White Supremacy and Racism in the Post-Civil Rights Era* (Boulder, Colo.: Lynne Reinner Publishers, 2001); Leslie G. Carr, *Color-Blind Racism* (Thousand Oaks, Calif.: Sage, 1997).

[19]Miroslav Volf, *Exclusion and Embrace: A Theological Exploration of Identity, Otherness and Reconciliation* (Nashville: Abingdon, 1996), p. 126.

[20]This is a cultural celebration that many Indian tribes still conduct today.

[21]My example of Sherelyn is not the end of the conversation about what corporate repentance will look like. If a critical core of European American Christians who are serious about corporate repentance would dialogue with Christians of color who are determined not to misuse their attitude of repentance, then we would have the sort of conversation we need to flesh out the practical dimensions of corporate repentance. For example, one of my white friends who reviewed this book at an

earlier stage observed that another important way corporate repentance can work itself out is through white Christians traveling and living in community with their brothers and sisters of color. This sort of connection will help white Christians understand past and contemporary forms of racism. Sherelyn, being married to a black man, has been a part of such a journey, and it comes out in her life. For example, when a black man was dragged to death behind a pickup truck in Jasper, Texas, she related to the incident not as just another tragic event but with the concern of a wife who fears her husband may be at risk.

[22]Michael O. Emerson and Christian Smith, *Divided by Faith: Evangelical Religion and the Problem of Race in America* (Oxford: Oxford University Press, 2000), p. 97.

Chapter 8: Sin Nature and Racial Minorities

[1]To see how racial minorities can become angry at the suggestion that whites can be victims of racism, read Joy James, *Shadowboxing: Representations of Black Feminist Politics* (New York: Palgrave Macmillan, 2002), and Frank Wu, *Yellow: Race in America Beyond Black and White* (New York: Basic Books, 2003).

[2]Miroslav Volf, *Exclusion and Embrace: A Theological Exploration of Identity, Otherness, and Reconciliation* (Nashville: Abingdon, 1996).

[3]Raleigh Washington and Glen Kehrein, *Breaking Down Walls: A Model for Reconciliation in an Age of Strife* (Chicago: Moody Press, 1993), p. 83.

[4]W. N. Brownsberger, "Race Matters: Disproportionality of Incarceration for Drug Dealing in Massachusetts," *Journal of Drug Issues* 30, no. 2 (2000): 345-74; R. S. Engel and J. M. Calnon, "Examining the Influence of Drivers' Characteristics During Traffic Stops with Police: Results from a National Survey," *Justice Quarterly* 21, no. 1 (2004): 49-90; A. J. Meehan and M. C. Ponder, "Race and Place: The Ecology of Racial Profiling African American Motorists," *Justice Quarterly* 19, no. 3 (2002): 399-430.

[5]The most famous example happened in 1994 when six African Americans filed a federal antidiscrimination lawsuit against Texaco. The lawsuit took on a life of its own when an angry employee secretly taped a meeting where some high-level executives made racist remarks. The episode has been used to indicate the degree of racism that exists in the upper levels of corporations.

[6]Monica Moorehead, "Reparations and Black Liberation," National Coalition of Blacks for Reparations, home page of NCOBRA, Washington, D.C., 2002 <www.ncobra.org>; Randall Robinson, *The Debt: What America Owes to Blacks* (New York: Penguin Putnam, 2000); R. Westley, "Many Billions Gone: Is It Time to Reconsider the Case for Black Reparations?" in *Should America Pay? Slavery and the Raging Debate on Reparations,* ed. Raymond A. Winbush (New York: Amistad, 2003).

[7]M. K. Asante, "The African American Warrant for Reparations: The Crime of Euro-

pean Enslavement of Africans and Its Consequences," in *Should America Pay?* ed. Winbush; Boris I. Bittker, *The Case for Black Reparations* (New York: Random House, 1973); Westley, "Many Billions Gone."

[8]Robinson, *The Debt;* Human Rights Watch, *An Approach to Reparations* (New York: Human Rights Watch, 2001); Westley, "Many Billions Gone."

[9]Westley, "Many Billions Gone."

[10]There is a biblical basis for individual restitution. In Leviticus 6:2-5 the Lord commands that anyone who cheats or steals from someone else must pay it back in its entirety plus a fifth of its value. When Zacchaeus put his faith in Christ, he pledged to pay back whatever he had stolen, four times over (Luke 19:8). So the idea of paying back what has been stolen is biblical. However, those are incidents of individual reparations. I am not sure there is a biblical case for corporate reparations, although it is an issue that theologians should take up.

[11]Estimates range from around 1 trillion dollars (Moorehead, "Reparations and Black Liberation") to 10 trillion dollars (J. Harper, "Bethune Puts the Issue on Trial," 2001 <www.blackvoices.com>). To get a concept of a trillion dollars, the estimated federal defense budget this year is only about 400 billion dollars. In fact our total estimated discretionary spending is only a little over 800 billion dollars. To pay off the 1 trillion dollar debt, the United States government would have to more than double its discretionary spending. Clearly, paying such an amount would have an adverse effect on our tax structure and would be felt by individual whites whom advocates of reparations claim not to want to saddle with this bill.

[12]Volf, *Exclusion and Embrace,* p. 126.

[13]Cornelius Plantinga Jr., *Not the Way It's Supposed to Be* (Grand Rapids: Eerdmans, 1995), pp. 9-12.

[14]Desmond Tutu, *No Future Without Forgiveness* (New York: Doubleday, 1999).

[15]In fact blacks have enslaved whites in our past. Accounts of Barbary slavery document the fact that blacks are capable of enslaving those of other races (Paul Baepler, *White Slaves, African Masters: An Anthology of American Barbary Captivity Narratives* [Chicago: University of Chicago Press, 1999]).

[16]It is tempting to imagine that Native Americans are morally superior to European Americans. Native Americans have not murdered majority group members to the same degree that majority group members have killed Indians. Yet when Indians had a brief military advantage over whites, they used the advantage to a cruel end. For example, Brown, in a book which is otherwise very sympathetic toward Native Americans, notes that Indians killed relatively defenseless settlers on the north side of the Minnesota River (Dee Brown, *Bury My Heart at Wounded Knee: An Indian History of the American West* [New York: Holt, Rinehart and Winston, 1971]). I point this out not to condemn Native people but to suggest that relative power rather than morality dictates how we treat each other. The degree of depravity differs be-

tween racial groups, but the depravity exists nevertheless.

[17]This is not to say that the buffalo soldiers had the same level of autonomy as the whites who ran the military units. It is tempting for us to excuse the buffalo soldiers because they were taking orders from white officers. But the excuse "I was just following orders" has never resonated well among those who are victimized.

Chapter 9: Jesus: The Ultimate Reconciler

[1]Millard Erickson convincingly argues that there is overwhelming evidence from Scripture that Jesus never sinned (Erickson, *Christian Theology*, 2nd ed. [Grand Rapids: Baker, 1998], pp. 735-37). For example, Jesus asked his accusers whether they had any evidence of sin (John 8:46), and no one could provide any. In several places the New Testament claims that Jesus was sinless (Matthew 27:19; John 8:29; 2 Corinthians 5:21; Hebrews 4:15; 1 Peter 2:22; 1 John 3:5). Perhaps the real question concerns the humanity of Jesus. If we define being human as being tempted and sinning, then does Jesus' sinless nature make him not human? I prefer to think that Jesus embodied what our human nature would be if it were not infected by sin. He was perfectly human, and we can learn to be fully human by reading about the actions of Jesus and doing our best to replicate those actions in our lives.

[2]I talk about ethnic differences and not racial ones because Roman society recognized ethnic divisions rather than racial differences.

[3]Craig L. Blomberg, *Jesus and the Gospels* (Nashville: Broadman & Holman, 1997).

[4]Ibid.

Chapter 10: The Fear Factor

[1]Howard Thurman, in his classic work *Jesus and the Disinherited*, accurately observed that marginalized individuals in society latch on to fear as a way to protect themselves from further disenfranchisement (Thurman, *Jesus and the Disinherited* [Boston: Beacon, 1976]). However, fear can soon destroy the internal self of societal victims. The sin of racism in our society may begin with external institutional discrimination, but it will soon infest our internal soul if we do not find ways to keep our fears in check.

[2]I have been asked which racial group has to change first if we are going to achieve racial healing. As in the marriage analogy, majority group members must change before they can reasonably expect changes from people of color. Nobody would expect a wife to become accountable to an abusive husband until he has undergone real repentance and counseling. Likewise people of color will not trust majority group members until they see genuine repentance. Like the wife, people of color have responsibilities to play in the reconstruction of the broken relationship, but without the initial repentance of the husband and majority group members, reconciliation can never get started. The mutual responsibility model requires corporate

repentance before corporate forgiveness.

[3]I think of two Christian books, each cowritten by a black and a white Christian who have created safe spaces to learn about racial reconciliation: Spencer Perkins and Chris Rice, More Than Equals: Racial Healing for the Sake of the Gospel (Downers Grove, Ill.: InterVarsity Press, 2000); and Raleigh Washington and Glen Kehrein, Breaking Down Walls: A Model for Reconciliation in an Age of Strife (Chicago: Moody Press, 1993).

[4]To see this assertion in the original, read Paul Kurtz, Humanist Manifesto I and II (Buffalo, N.Y.: Prometheus, 1973).

[5]R. Farley et al., "Stereotypes and Segregation: Neighborhoods in the Detroit Area," American Journal of Sociology 100 (1994): 750-80; M. Jackman and M. J. Mahu, "Education and Intergroup Attitudes: Moral Enlightenment, Superficial Democratic Commitment or Ideological Refinement?" American Sociological Review 49 (1984): 751-69.

[6]In fact a paper written by two of my colleagues indicates that whites with a higher level of education are more likely than those with less education to act in ways that promote residential and educational racial segregation (Michael Emerson and D. H. Sikkink, "White Attitudes, White Actions: Education and the Reproduction of a Racialized Society" [paper presented at the American Sociological Association Meetings, San Francisco, 1998]). Their actions occurred despite the fact that they were less likely to indicate a preference for segregation.

[7]Perkins and Rice, More Than Equals.

[8]George Yancey, Beyond Black and White: Reflections on Racial Reconciliation (Grand Rapids: Baker, 1996), pp. 13-15.

Chapter 11: What Would a Christian Solution Look Like?

[1]Thomas Edsall and Mary D. Edsall, Chain Reaction: The Impact of Race, Rights, and Taxes on American Politics (New York: Norton, 1991); Andrew Hacker, Two Nations: Black and White, Separate, Hostile, and Unequal (New York: Ballantine, 1995); Howard Schuman et al., Racial Attitudes in America: Trends and Interpretations (Cambridge, Mass.: Harvard University Press, 1997).

[2]I might disagree with other aspects of Bill Clinton's presidency, but I think that his admonition that we should "mend it and not end it" may be the closest any politician has come to an authentic Christian statement about affirmative action.

[3]Perhaps when the Bible talks about being a slave to sin (John 8:34-36; Romans 6:16-18; Galatians 4:7-8), it tells us one implication of our slavery is that we are unable to see beyond our own selfish needs to find solutions that will benefit the entire society.

[4]Curtiss Paul DeYoung et al., United By Faith: The Multiracial Church as an Answer to the Problem of Race (Oxford: Oxford University Press, 2003).

5George Yancey, *One Body, One Spirit: Principles of Successful Multiracial Churches* (Downers Grove, Ill.: InterVarsity Press, 2003).

6Multiracial churches were those where at least one of the main services was not more than 80 percent of a given race. If we had applied a more stringent standard for whether a church is multiracial, the percentage would be even lower.

7One of the characteristics of multiracial churches seemed to be that they took less extreme political stances than other churches (P. E. Becker, "Making Inclusive Communities: Congregations and the 'Problem' of Race," *Social Problems* 45, no. 4 [1998]: 451-72). It is possible that members of multiracial churches prefer to emphasize the unity of their faith and perceive secular political differences as nonessential issues.

8Yancey, *One Body, One Spirit.*

9M. T. Hallinan and R. A. Teixeira, "Opportunities and Constraints: Black-White Differences in the Formation of Interracial Friendships," *Child Development* 58, no. 5 (1987): 1358-71; J. Moody, "Race, School Integration, and Friendship Segregation in America," *American Journal of Sociology* 107, no. 3 (2001): 679-716.

10M. Jackman and M. Crane, "'Some of My Best Friends Are Black . . .': Interracial Friendship and Whites' Racial Attitudes," *Public Opinion Quarterly* 50 (1986): 459-86; Kathleen O. Korgen, *Crossing the Racial Divide: Close Friendships Between Black and White Americans* (Westport, Conn.: Praeger, 2002).

11I am researching possible effects on racial attitudes of those who marry interracially. At present the results are promising. It may be possible that marital relationships contain an intimacy which shapes racial attitudes in a way that nonromantic relationships are unable to do.

12George Yancey, "Rubbing Off on Each Other: Close Interracial Friendships, Integrated Friendship Networks and Racial Attitudes," unpublished paper.

13Some fear that people of color will become unduly influenced by their white friends and lose their drive for racial justice. However, my research has indicated that people of color who attend multiracial churches (Yancey, "Racial Attitudes: Differences in Racial Attitudes of People Attending Multiracial and Uniracial Congregations," *Research in the Social Scientific Study of Religion* 12 [2001]) or who are interracially married (Yancey, "Ethnocultural Allodynia or White Ignorance? How Multiracial Couples Deal with Contrasting Racial Realities" [paper presented at the National Association for Ethnic Studies, Chicago, 2005]) have basically the same racial attitudes as other people of color.

14Others may be called to do more than merely seek out those of different races who are naturally in their path and need to take the radical step of relocating to be near racial diversity. It is up to you to decide if this is what the Lord wants for you, but I believe that more white Christians should resist white flight. Likewise I believe that more Christians of color should question the type of ethnocentrism which discourages them from joining majority group dominated social institutions.

[15]Michael O. Emerson, R. T. Kimbro and George Yancey, "Contact Theory Extended: The Effects of Prior Racial Contact on Current Social Ties," *Social Science Quarterly* 83, no. 3 (2002): 745-61.

[16]For example, Bai and Isikoff document that 90 percent of all African Americans supported Al Gore for president in 2000 (M. Bai and M. Isikoff, "Clouds over the Sunshine State," *Newsweek*, November 20, 2000, pp. 16-25). It is hard to see how any other group would have such a degree of loyalty to the Democratic Party.

[17]Michael O. Emerson and Christian Smith, *Divided by Faith: Evangelical Religion and the Problem of Race in America* (Oxford: Oxford University Press, 2000).

[18]Kristin Luker, *Abortion and the Politics of Motherhood* (Berkeley: University of California Press, 1985); Ralph Reed, "Casting a Wider Net," *Policy Review* 65 (1993): 31-35.

[19]This is generally true of minority Christians who are not officeholders. Minority Democrats who are officeholders are very likely to support abortion. However, research has indicated that blacks and Hispanics are more likely than whites to be prolife (E. J. Hall and M. M. Ferree, "Race Differences in Abortion Attitudes," *Public Opinion Quarterly* 50 (1986): 193-207; T. W. Smith, *Public Opinion on Abortion* (Chicago: National Opinion Research Center, 1998).

[20]B. Christerson and P. Menjares, "Race and Religion at an Evangelical College: An In-Depth Case Study" (paper presented at the Society for the Scientific Study of Religion, Salt Lake City, Utah, November 2002).

[21]C. J. Gardner, "Keeping Students in School," *Christianity Today* 42 (1998): 34-36.

[22]In my personal conversations with Brad Christerson, a Christian sociologist who has studied students at a Christian college, he indicated that Christian students are willing to think more deeply about racial issues if they are given scriptural reasons for doing so. If he is correct, then we also have to look at the responsibility of Christian theologians to provide us with ammunition to shoot down our reliance on failed secular models.

References

Anderson, Brian C. "Secular Europe, Religious America." *Public Interest* 155 (2004): 143-58.

Anderson, Claud. *Black Labor, White Wealth: The Search for Power and Economic Justice.* Bethesda, Md.: Powernomics Corporation in America, 1994.

Anderson, Elijah. *Streetwise: Race, Class and Change in an Urban Community.* Chicago: University of Chicago Press, 1990.

Ansell, Amy E. *New Right, New Racism: Race and Reaction in the United States and Britain.* Washington Square: New York University Press, 1997.

Anstey, Roger. "A Re-interpretation of the Abolition of the British Slave Trade, 1806-1807." *The English Historical Review* 87, no. 343 (1972): 304-32.

Asante, Molefi Kete. "The African American Warrant for Reparations: The Crime of European Enslavement of Africans and Its Consequences." In *Should America Pay? Slavery and the Raging Debate on Reparations,* edited by Raymond Winbush. New York: Amistad, 2003.

Athanases, Steven, David Christiano and Elizabeth Lay. "Fostering Empathy and Finding Common Ground in Multiethnic Classes." *English Journal* 84 (1995): 26-34.

Baepler, Paul. *White Slaves, African Masters: An Anthology of American Barbary Captivity Narratives.* Chicago: University of Chicago Press, 1999.

Bai, Matt, and Michael Isikoff. "Clouds over the Sunshine State." *Newsweek,* November 20, 2000, pp. 16-25.

Bak, Hans. "The Health Is On: Canon or Kaleidoscope." In *Multiculturalism and the Canon of American Culture,* edited by Hans Bak, pp. 65-80. Amsterdam: VU University Press, 1993.

Bank, James. *Teaching Strategies for Ethnic Studies.* Boston: Allyn and Bacon, 1987.

Barndt, Joseph. *Dismantling Racism: The Continuing Challenge to White America.* Minneapolis: Augsburg Fortress, 1991.

Becker, Penny E. "Making Inclusive Communities: Congregations and the 'Problem' of Race." *Social Problems* 45, no. 4 (1998): 451-72.

Bellah, Robert N., Richard Madsen, William M. Sullivan, Ann Swidler and Steven M. Tipton. *Habits of the Heart: Individualism and Commitment in American Life.* Berkeley: University of California Press, 1985.

Bennett, William J. *The Devaluing of America.* Nashville: Thomas Nelson, 1994.

Berryman, Phillip. *Liberation Theology.* New York: Pantheon, 1987.

Billingsley, Andrew. *Black Families in White America.* Englewood Cliffs, N.J.: Prentice-Hall, 1968.

Bittker, Boris I. *The Case for Black Reparations.* New York: Random House, 1973.

Blassingame, John W. *The Slave Community: Plantation Life in the Antebellum South.* New York: Oxford University Press, 1972.

Blomberg, Craig L. *Jesus and the Gospels.* Nashville: Broadman & Holman, 1997.

Bobo, Lawrence, James R. Kluegel and Ryan A. Smith. "Laissez-Faire Racism: The Crystallization of a Kinder, Gentler, Antiblack Ideology." In *Racial Attitudes in the 1990s: Continuity and Change,* edited by Steven

A. Tuch and Jack K. Martin, pp. 15-42. Westport, Conn.: Praeger, 1997.

Bobo, Lawrence, and Ryan A. Smith. "From Jim Crow Racism to Laissez-Faire Racism: The Transformation of Racial Attitudes." In *Beyond Pluralism: The Conception of Groups and Group Identities in America*, edited by Wendy F. Katkin, Ned Landsman and Andrea Tyree. Urbana: University of Illinois Press, 1998.

Boff, Leonardo, and Clodovis Boff. *Introducing Liberation Theology.* Maryknoll, N.Y.: Orbis, 1987.

Bogin, Ruth, and Jean Fagan Yellin. Introduction to *The Abolition Sisterhood: Women's Political Culture in Antebellum America,* edited by J. F. Yellin and J. C. Van Horne. Ithaca, N.Y.: Cornell University Press, 1994.

Bonacich, Edna. "A Theory of Ethnic Antagonism: The Split Labor Market." *American Sociological Review* 37 (October 1972): 547-59.

Bonilla-Silva, Eduardo. "Rethinking Racism: Towards a Structural Interpretation." *American Sociological Review* 62 (1997): 465-80.

———. *White Supremacy and Racism in the Post-Civil Rights Era.* Boulder, Colo.: Lynne Rienner Publishers, 2001.

Bonilla-Silva, Eduardo, and Amanda Lewis. "The 'New Racism': Toward an Analysis of the U.S. Racial Structure, 1960s-1990s." In *Race, Ethnicity and Nationality in the United States: Toward the Twenty-First Century,* edited by Paul Wong. Boulder, Colo.: Westview Press, 1998.

Boyd, Julia A. *In the Company of My Sisters: Black Women and Self-Esteem.* New York: Dutton Books, 1993.

Boyle, Elizabeth H. *Female Genital Cutting: Cultural Conflict in the Global Community.* Baltimore: Johns Hopkins University Press, 2002.

Bradley, Anthony. "A New Division, a New Dream." *World* 16, no. 56 (2001).

Brown, Dee. *Bury My Heart at Wounded Knee: An Indian History of the American West.* New York: Holt, Rinehart and Winston, 1971.

Brownsberger, William N. "Race Matters: Disproportionality of Incarceration for Drug Dealing in Massachusetts." *Journal of Drug Issues* 30, no. 2 (2000): 345-74.

Carmichael, Stokely, and Charles V. Hamilton. *Black Power: The Politics of Liberation in America.* New York: Vintage Books, 1967.

Carr, Leslie G. *Color-Blind Racism.* Thousand Oaks, Calif.: Sage, 1997.

Carr-Rufino, Norma. *Managing Diversity: People Skills for a Multicultural Workplace.* Boston: Pearson Custom Publishers, 2002.

Cassidy, Michael. *The Passing Summer.* Ventura, Calif.: Regal Books, 1989.

Chandler, Paul-Gordon. *God's Global Mosaic: What We Can Learn from Christians Around the World.* Downers Grove, Ill.: InterVarsity Press, 2000.

Cherlin, Andrew J. *Marriage, Divorce, Remarriage.* Cambridge, Mass.: Harvard University Press, 1992.

Christerson, Brad, and Pete Menjares. "Race and Religion at an Evangelical College: An In-Depth Case Study." Paper presented at the Society for the Scientific Study of Religion, Salt Lake City, Utah, November 2002.

Citron, Abraham F. *The Rightness of Whiteness: The World of the White Child in a Segregated Society.* Detroit: Michigan-Ohio Regional Educational Laboratory, 1969.

Clark, Kenneth B. *Dark Ghetto: Dilemmas of Social Power.* New York: Harper, 1965.

Clark, William A. V. "Residential Preferences and Neighborhood Racial Segregation: A Test of the Schelling Segregation Model." *Demography* 28 (1991): 1-19.

Cohen, Carl I., Kathryn Hyland and Carol Magai. "Depression Among African American Nursing Home Patients with Dementia." *American Journal of Psychiatry* 6 (1998):162-75.

Cole, David. *No Equal Justice: Race and Class in the American Criminal Justice System.* New York: New Press, 2000.

Colson, Charles. *Loving God.* Grand Rapids: Zondervan, 1997.

Conde-Frazier, Elizabeth, S. Steve Kang and Gary A. Parrett. *A Many Colored Kingdom: Multicultural Dynamics for Spiritual Formation.* Grand Rapids: Baker, 2004.

Cone, James H. *Black Theology and Black Power.* New York: Seabury, 1969.

Congress, Elaine, ed. *Multicultural Perspectives in Working with Families.* New York: Springer, 1997.

Connerly, Ward. *Creating Equal: My Fight Against Race Preferences.* San Francisco: Encounter Books, 2000.

Cox, Taylor. *Creating the Multicultural Organization: A Strategy for Capturing the Power of Diversity.* San Francisco: Jossey-Bass, 2001.

Dalton, Harlon. "Failing to See." In *White Privilege: Essential Readings on the Other Side of Racism,* edited by Paula S. Rothenberg, pp. 15-18. New York: Worth, 2002.

Daniels, Celia. "Black Racist: The Debate Continues." *Community Contact* 7 (1998): 4.

DeBlassie, Adele M., and Richard R. DeBlassie. "Education of Hispanic Youth: A Cultural Lag." *Adolescence* 31, no. 121 (1996): 205-16.

Delgado, Richard, and Jean Stefancic. *Critical Race Theory: An Introduction.* New York: New York University Press, 2001.

Delk, Yvonne. "A Time for Action: Building Strategy to Dismantle Racism." *Sojourners* 27 (1998): 25.

Delpit, Lisa D. *Other People's Children: Cultural Conflict in the Classroom.* New York: New Press, 1996.

Denton, Nancy, and Douglas S. Massey. "Residential Segregation of Blacks, Hispanics, and Asians by Socioeconomic Status and Generation." *Social Science Quarterly* 69 (1988): 797-817.

DeYoung, Curtiss Paul. *Coming Together: The Bible's Message in an Age of Diversity.* Valley Forge, Penn.: Judson Press, 1995.

DeYoung, Curtiss Paul, Michael O. Emerson, George Yancey and Karen

Chai Kim. *United by Faith: The Multiracial Church as an Answer to the Problem of Race.* Oxford: Oxford University Press, 2003.

Dobson, James. *The Complete Marriage and Family Home Reference Guide.* Carol Stream, Ill.: Tyndale House, 2000.

Donner, James K. "Learning from Black Folks." In *Critical Race Theory Perspectives on the Social Studies: The Profession, Policies, and Curriculum,* edited by G. Ladson-Billing. Greenwich, Conn.: Information Age Publishing, 2003.

Dovidio, John. "The Subtlety of Racism." *Training and Development* 47, no. 4 (1993): 51-57.

D'Souza, Dinesh. *The End of Racism: Principles for a Multiracial Society.* New York: Free Press, 1996.

DuBois, W. E. B. *The Soul of Black Folks.* New York: Dover Publications, 1994.

Dyson, Michael E. *I May Not Get There with You: The True Martin Luther King Jr.* New York: Free Press, 2001.

Eastland, Terry, and William J. Bennett. *Counting by Race: Equality from the Founding Fathers to Bakke and Weber.* New York: Basic Books, 1979.

Edsall, Thomas, with Mary D. Edsall. *Chain Reaction: The Impact of Race, Rights, and Taxes on American Politics.* New York: Norton, 1991.

Elizondo, V. "Benevolent Tolerance or Humble Reverence? A Vision for Multicultural Religious Education." In *Multicultural Religious Education,* edited by Barbara Wilkerson, pp. 395-405. Birmingham, Ala.: Religious Education Press, 1997.

Elkins, Stanley. *Slavery.* 2nd ed. Chicago: University of Chicago Press, 1968.

Elliott, Harrison S. *Can Religious Education Be Christian?* New York: Macmillan, 1940.

Emerson, Michael O., and Christian Smith. *Divided by Faith: Evangelical Religion and the Problem of Race in America.* Oxford: Oxford University Press, 2000.

Emerson, Michael O., and David H. Sikkink. "White Attitudes, White Actions: Education and the Reproduction of a Racialized Society." Paper presented at the American Sociological Association Meetings, San Francisco, 1998.

Emerson, Michael O., George Yancey and Karen Chai Kim. "Does Race Matter in Residential Segregation? Exploring the Preferences of White Americans." *American Sociological Review* 6 (2001): 922-35.

Emerson, Michael O., Rachel T. Kimbro and George Yancey. "Contact Theory Extended: The Effects of Prior Racial Contact on Current Social Ties." *Social Science Quarterly* 83, no. 3 (2002): 745-61.

Engel, Robin Shepard, and Jennifer M. Calnon. "Examining the Influence of Drivers' Characteristics During Traffic Stops with Police: Results from a National Survey." *Justice Quarterly* 21, no. 1 (2004): 49-90.

Epstein, Lee, and Joseph F. Kobylka. *The Supreme Court and Legal Change.* Chapel Hill: University of North Carolina Press, 1992.

Erickson, Millard J. *Christian Theology.* 2nd ed. Grand Rapids: Baker, 1998.

Evans, John H. "Polarization in Abortion Attitudes in U.S. Religious Traditions, 1972-1998." *Sociological Forum* 17, no. 3 (2002): 397-422.

Farley, Reynolds. "Residential Segregation in Urbanized Areas in the United States in 1970: An Analysis of Social Class and Racial Differences." *Demography* 14 (1977): 497-518.

Farley, Reynolds, Charlotte Steeh, Maria Krysan, Tara Jackson and Keith Reeves. "Stereotypes and Segregation: Neighborhoods in the Detroit Area." *American Journal of Sociology* 100 (1994): 750-80.

Feagin, Joe R. *Racist America: Roots, Current Realities, and Future Reparations.* New York: Routledge, 2000.

Federal Glass Ceiling Commission. *Good for Business: Making Full Use of the Nation's Human Capital.* Washington, D.C.: U.S. Government Printing Office, 1995.

Finnie, Gordon E. "The Antislavery Movement in the Upper South Before 1840." *The Journal of Southern History* 35, no. 3 (1969): 319-42.

Fletcher, Joseph. *Situation Ethics: The New Morality.* Louisville, Ky.: Westminster John Knox Press, 1997.

Frame, Randy. "Helping the Poor Help Themselves." *Christianity Today,* February 3, 1997, pp. 70-73.

Free, Marvin D., Jr. *African Americans and the Criminal Justice System.* New York: Garland, 1995.

Fuller, Jonathan H. S., and P. D. Toon. *Medical Practice in a Multicultural Society.* Woburn, Mass.: Butterworth-Heinemann Medical, 1988.

Gaede, Stan D. *When Tolerance Is No Virtue: Political Correctness, Multiculturalism and the Future of Truth and Justice.* Downers Grove, Ill.: InterVarsity Press, 1993.

Gallagher, Charles, "Racial Redistricting: Expanding the Boundaries of Whiteness." In *The Politics of Multiracialism,* edited by Heather M. Dalmage. New York: State University of New York Press, 2004.

Gallup, George J., Jr., and D. Michael Lindsay. *Surveying the Religious Landscape: Trends in U.S. Beliefs.* Harrisburg, Penn.: Morehouse Publishing, 1999.

Gardner, Christine J. "Keeping Students in School." *Christianity Today* 42 (1998): 34-36.

Gellner, Ernest. *Nations and Nationalism.* Oxford: Blackwell, 1983.

Glazer, Nathan. *We Are All Multiculturalists Now.* Cambridge, Mass.: Harvard University Press, 1998.

Gonzalez, Justo L., and Catherine G. Gonzalez. *Liberation Preaching: The Pulpit and the Oppressed.* Nashville: Abingdon, 1980.

Gutierrez, Gustavo. *A Theology of Liberation: History, Politics and Salvation.* Maryknoll, N.Y.: Orbis, 1973.

Hacker, Andrew. *Two Nations: Black and White, Separate, Hostile, and Unequal.* New York: Ballantine, 1995.

Hall, Elaine J., and Myra M. Ferree. "Race Differences in Abortion Attitudes." *Public Opinion Quarterly* 50 (1986): 193-207.

Hallinan, Maureen T., and Ruy A. Teixeira. "Opportunities and Constraints: Black-White Differences in the Formation of Interracial Friendships." *Child Development* 58, no. 5 (1987): 1358-71.

Han, John J. "The Uses of Reading Ethnic Minority Literature: The Christian Multiculturalism." Paper presented at the National Faculty Leadership Conference, Chicago, 2001.

Harman, Allan. "Racism in Australia." *Theological Forum* 25 (1997): 4.

Harper, James. "Bethune Puts the Issue on Trial." (2001). Accessed at <www.blackvoices.com> .

Henry, Jonathan, Shaw Fuller and P. D. Toon. *Medical Practice in a Multicultural Society.* Burlington, Mass.: Butterworth-Heinemann, 1988.

Henry, William A. "Beyond the Melting Pot." *Time*, April 9, 1990, pp. 28-31.

Hertel, Bradley R., and Michael Hughes. "Religious Affiliation, Attendance, and Support for 'Pro-Family' Issues in the United States." *Social Forces* 65, no. 3 (1987): 858-82.

Hilliard, A. G. "Conceptual Confusion and the Persistence of Group Oppression Through Education." *Equity and Excellence* 24, no. 1 (1988): 36-43.

Hochschild, Jennifer L. *Facing Up to the American Dream: Race, Class and the Soul of the Nation.* Princeton, N.J.: Princeton University Press, 1995.

Horowitz, David, and Jamie Glazov. *Left Illusions: An Intellectual Odyssey.* Dallas: Spence, 2003.

Howard, Gary R. *We Can't Teach What We Don't Know: White Teachers, Multiracial Schools.* New York: Teacher College Press, 1999.

Hu-DeHart, Evelyn. "Rethinking America: The Practice of Politics of Multiculturalism in Higher Education." In *Beyond a Dream Deferred: Multicultural Education and the Politics of Excellence,* edited by Becky W. Thompson and Sangeeta Tyagi. Minneapolis: University of Minnesota Press, 1993.

Human Rights Watch. *An Approach to Reparations.* New York: Human Rights Watch, 2001.

Irvine, Jacqueline J. *Black Students and School Failure: Policies, Practices, and Prescriptions.* Westport, Conn.: Praeger, 1991.

Jackman, Mary, and Marie Crane. "'Some of My Best Friends Are Black . . .': Interracial Friendship and Whites' Racial Attitudes." *Public Opinion Quarterly* 50 (1986): 459-86.

Jackman, Mary, and Michael J. Mahu. "Education and Intergroup Attitudes: Moral Enlightenment, Superficial Democratic Commitment or Ideological Refinement?" *American Sociological Review* 49 (1984): 751-69.

James, Joy. *Shadowboxing: Representations of Black Feminist Politics.* New York: Palgrave Macmillan, 2002.

Jones, Bob, IV. "Mrs. Taylor's Neighborhood." *World,* May 16, 1998, p. 13.

Kellas, James G. *The Politics of Nationalism and Ethnicity.* New York: St. Martin's Press, 1991.

Kenton, Sherron B., and Deborah Valentine. *Crosstalk: Communicating in a Multicultural Workplace.* Upper Saddle River, N.J.: Prentice Hall, 1996.

Kinder, Donald R., and Lynn M. Sanders. *Divided by Color: Racial Politics and Democratic Ideals.* Chicago: University of Chicago Press, 1996.

King, Martin Luther, Jr. *Why We Can't Wait.* New York: New American Library, 2000.

Kisubi, Alfred T. "Ideological Perspectives on Multiculturalism." In *Multiculturalism in a Cross-National Perspective,* edited by Michael Burayidi, pp. 15-35. Lanham, Md.: University Press of America, 1997.

Kluegel, J. R. "Trends in Whites' Explanation of the Black-White Gap in Socioeconomic Status, 1977-1989." *American Sociological Review* 55 (1990): 512-25.

Koppelman, Kent L., and R. Lee Goodhart. *Understanding Human Differences: Multicultural Education for a Diverse America.* Boston: Pearson Education, 2005.

Korgen, Kathleen Odell. *Crossing the Racial Divide: Close Friendships Between Black and White Americans.* Westport, Conn.: Praeger, 2002.

Kozol, Jonathan. *Savage Inequalities: Children in America's Schools.* New York: Crown, 1991.

Kunjufu, Jawanza. *Countering the Conspiracy to Destroy Black Boys.* Chicago: African American Images, 1990.

Kurtz, Paul. *Humanist Manifesto I and II.* Buffalo: Prometheus, 1973.

Ladson-Billing, Gloria. "Lies My Teacher Still Tells." In *Critical Race Theory Perspectives on Social Studies: The Profession, Policies, and Curriculum,* edited by Gloria Ladson-Billing. Greenwich, Conn.: Information Age Publishing, 2003.

Lake, Robert. *The New Suburbanites: Race and Housing in the Suburbs.* New Brunswick, N.J.: Rutgers University Center for Urban Policy Research, 1981.

Lewis, C. S. *The Screwtape Letters.* New York: Macmillan, 1976.

Lewis, Oscar. *Five Families: Mexican Case Studies in the Culture of Poverty.* New York: Basic Books, 1959.

————. *La Vida: A Puerto Rican Family in the Culture of Poverty—San Juan and New York.* New York: Random House, 1965.

Limbaugh, David. "Race-Based Preferences Harm Society." *WorldNetDaily,* March 30, 2001 <www.worldnetdaily.com/news/article.asp?ARTICLE_ID=22237>.

Luker, Kristin. *Abortion and the Politics of Motherhood.* Berkeley: University of California Press, 1985.

Manning, Marable. "Racism and Multicultural Democracy." In *Double Exposure: Poverty and Race in America,* edited by C. Hartman, pp. 151-60. Armonk, N.Y.: M. E. Sharp, 1997.

Martin, Asa E. "Pioneer Anti-Slavery Press." *The Mississippi Valley Historical Review* 2, no. 4 (1916): 509-28.

Massey, Douglas S., and Nancy A. Denton. *American Apartheid: Segrega-*

tion and the Making of the Underclass. Cambridge, Mass.: Harvard University Press, 1996.

Maxwell, Nan L. "The Effects on Black-White Wage Differences in the Quantity and Quality of Education." *Industrial and Labor Relations Review* 47, no. 2 (1994): 249-65.

McConahay, John B. "Modern Racism, Ambivalence, and the Modern Racism Scale." In *Prejudice, Discrimination, and Racism: Theory and Research,* edited by John S. Dovidio and Samuel L. Gaertner. New York: Academic Press, 1986.

McGee, Robert S. *The Search for Significance: Seeing Your True Worth Through God's Eyes.* Nashville: W. Publishing Group, 1998.

McIntosh, Peggy. "White Privilege: Unpacking the Invisible Knapsack." In *White Privilege: Essential Readings on the Other Side of Racism,* edited by Paula S. Rothenberg, pp. 97-102. New York: Worth, 2002.

McLaren, Peter. "White Terror and Oppositional Agency: Towards a Critical Multiculturalism." In *Multiculturalism: A Critical Reader,* edited by David T. Goldberg, pp. 45-74. Malden, Mass.: Blackwell Publishers, 1994.

McLemore, S. Dale, Harriet D. Romo and Susan G. Baker. *Racial and Ethnic Relations in America.* Boston, Mass.: Allyn and Bacon, 2001.

McMinn, Mark R. *Why Sin Matters: The Surprising Relationship Between Our Sin and God's Grace.* Wheaton, Ill.: Tyndale House, 2004.

Meehan, Albert J., and Michael C. Ponder. "Race and Place: The Ecology of Racial Profiling African American Motorists." *Justice Quarterly* 19, no. 3 (2002): 399-430.

Miller, John J. *The Unmaking of Americans: How Multiculturalism Has Undermined America's Assimilation Ethic.* New York: Simon and Schuster, 1998.

Mintz, Sidney W. "Slavery and Emergent Capitalisms." In *Slavery in the New World,* edited by Laura Foner and Eugene D. Genovese. Englewood Cliffs, N.J.: Prentice-Hall, 1969.

Moody, James. "Race, School Integration, and Friendship Segregation in America." *American Journal of Sociology* 107, no. 3 (2001): 679-716.

Moorehead, Monica. "Reparations and Black Liberation." *Workers World Newspaper* 44 (2002): 1, 7.

Moran, Rachel F. *Interracial Intimacy: The Regulation of Race and Romance.* Chicago: University of Chicago Press, 2001.

Morris, Leon. *New Testament Theology.* Grand Rapids: Zondervan, 1990.

Moynihan, Daniel Patrick. *The Negro Family.* Washington, D.C.: U.S. Department of Labor, 1965.

Myrdal, Gunnar. *An American Dilemma: The Negro Problem and Modern Democracy.* New York: McGraw-Hill, 1964.

Neff, David. "Dare We Be Colorblind?" *Christianity Today,* February 3, 1997, pp. 14-15.

Newman, William. *American Pluralism.* New York: Harper & Row, 1973.

Nicklin, Julie L. "Helping to Manage Diversity in the Workforce." *Chronicle of Higher Education,* September 30, 1992, p. A5.

Niebuhr, Reinhold. *The Nature and Destiny of Man.* New York: Scribner's Sons, 1941.

Nieto, Sonia. *Affirming Diversity: The Sociopolitical Context of Multicultural Education.* 3rd ed. Boston: Allyn and Bacon, 1999.

Noll, Mark A. *A History of Christianity in the United States and Canada.* Grand Rapids: Eerdmans, 1992.

Oliver, Melvin L., and Thomas M. Shapiro. *Black Wealth/White Wealth: A New Perspective on Racial Inequality.* New York: Routledge, 1995.

Pachen, Martin. *Diversity and Unity: Relations Between Racial Ethnic Groups.* Chicago: Nelson-Hall Publishers, 1999.

Pannell, William E. *The Coming Race Wars? A Cry for Reconciliation.* Grand Rapids: Zondervan, 1993.

Parker, Star. *Pimps, Whores and Welfare Brats: From Welfare Cheat to Conservative Messenger.* New York: Pocket Books, 1998.

Perkins, Spencer, and Chris Rice. *More Than Equals: Racial Healing for the*

Sake of the Gospel. Downers Grove, Ill.: InterVarsity Press, 2000.

Plantinga, Cornelius, Jr. *Not the Way It's Supposed to Be.* Grand Rapids: Eerdmans, 1995.

Popenoe, David. *Disturbing the Nest: Family Change and Decline in Modern Societies.* New York: Aldine de Gruyter, 1988.

Pyne, Robert A. *Humanity and Sin: The Creation, Fall and Redemption of Humanity.* Nashville: Word, 1999.

Rahman, Anika, and Nahid Toubia, editors. *Female Genital Mutilation: A Practical Guide to Worldwide Laws and Policies.* Vol. 3. London: Zed Books, 2000.

Reed, Ralph. "Casting a Wider Net." *Policy Review* 65 (1993): 31-35.

————. *Active Faith: How Christians Are Changing the Soul of American Politics.* New York: Free Press, 1996.

Reich, Michael. "The Political-Economic Effects of Racism." In *The Capitalist System: A Radical Analysis of American Society.* 3rd ed., edited by Richard C. Edwards, Michael Reich and Thomas E. Weisskopf. Englewood Cliffs, N.J.: Prentice-Hall, 1986.

Robinson, Randall. *The Debt: What America Owes to Blacks.* New York: Penguin Putman, 2000.

Rothenberg, Paula S., editor. *White Privilege: Essential Readings on the Other Side of Racism.* New York: Worth, 2002.

Ryan, William. *Blaming the Victim.* New York: Random House, 1976.

Salter-McNeil, Brenda, and Rick Richardson. *The Heart of Racial Justice: How Soul Change Leads to Social Change.* Downers Grove, Ill.: InterVarsity Press, 2005.

Schiele, Jerome. "Afrocentricity: Implications for Higher Education." *Journal of Black Studies* 25, no. 2 (1994): 150-69.

Schneider, Barbara, and Yongsook Lee. "A Model for Academic Success: The School and Home Environment of East Asian Students." *Anthropology and Education Quarterly* 21 (December 1990): 358-77.

Schuman, Howard, Charlotte Steeh, Lawrence Bobo and Maria Krysan.

Racial Attitudes in America: Trends and Interpretations. Cambridge, Mass.: Harvard University Press, 1997.

Sears, David O. "Symbolic Racism." In *Eliminating Racism,* edited by Phyllis A. Katz and Dalmas A. Taylor. New York: Plenum, 1988.

Shrewsbury, Prisca. "No Qualifiers Needed: Turning Down the Ironic Insult of Racial Preference." *World* 18 (2003).

Shuler, Clarence. *Winning the Race to Unity: Is Racial Reconciliation Really Working?* Chicago: Moody Press, 2003.

Sidanius, J., F. Pratto and L. Bobo. "Racism, Conservatism, Affirmative Action, and Intellectual Sophistication: A Matter of Principled Conservatism or Group Dominance?" *Journal of Personality and Social Psychology* 70, no. 3 (1996): 476-90.

Sider, Ronald J. *Rich Christians in an Age of Hunger: A Biblical Study.* Downers Grove, Ill.: InterVarsity Press, 1978.

Silko, Leslie M. *Storyteller.* New York: Arcade, 1989.

Sillars, L. "Unaffirmative Action: Black Vendor Sues 'Racist' City Program." *World* 14 (1999): 23.

Sleeter, Christine, and Carl Grant. *Making Choices for Multicultural Education.* 3rd ed. New York: Merrill, 1999.

Smith, Tom W. *Public Opinion on Abortion.* Chicago: National Opinion Research Center, 1998.

Sowell, Thomas. *Race and Culture: A World View.* New York: Basic Books, 1995.

Spencer, Martin E. "Multiculturalism, Political Correctness and the Politics of Identity." *Sociological Forum* 9 (December 1994): 547-67.

Steele, Shelby. *The Content of Our Character: A New Vision of Race in America.* New York: St. Martin's Press, 1990.

Steinberg, Laurence. *Beyond the Classroom.* New York: Simon and Schuster, 1997.

Strickler, James A., and Nicholas L. Danigelis. "Changing Frameworks in Attitudes Toward Abortion." *Sociological Forum* 17, no. 2 (2002): 187-201.

Sweet, James A., and Larry L. Bumpass. *American Families and Households*. New York: Russell Sage Foundation, 1987.

Swerdlow, Amy. "Abolition's Conservative Sisters: The Ladies' New York City Anti-Slavery Societies, 1834-1840." In *The Abolitionist Sisterhood: Women's Political Culture in Antebellum America*, edited by Jean F. Yellin and John C. Van Horne. Ithaca, N.Y.: Cornell University Press, 1994.

Szymanski, Albert. "Racial Discrimination and White Gain." *American Sociological Review* 41 (1976): 403-14.

Takaki, Ronald. *A Different Mirror: A History of Multicultural America*. Boston: Little, Brown, 1994.

Taylor, Charles. "The Politics of Recognition." In *Multiculturalism: A Critical Reader,* edited by David T. Goldberg, pp. 75-106. Malden, Mass.: Blackwell Publishers, 1994.

Tennant, Frederick R. *The Origin and Propagation of Sin*. Cambridge: Cambridge University Press, 1902.

Thernstrom, Stephen. *America in Black and White: One Nation, Indivisible*. New York: Simon & Schuster, 1999.

Thomas, Alexander, and Samuel Sillen. *Racism and Psychiatry*. New York: Bruner-Mazel, 1972.

Thurman, Howard. *Jesus and the Disinherited*. Boston: Beacon, 1976.

Tie, Warwick. *Legal Pluralism: Toward a Multicultural Conception of Law*. Brookfield, Vt.: Dartmouth Publishing, 1999.

Trotman, C. James. Introduction. In *Multiculturalism: Roots and Realities,* edited by C. James Trotman, pp. ix-xvii. Bloomington: Indiana University Press, 2002.

Turnbull, Joanne E., and Ada Mui. "Mental Health Status and Needs of Black and White Elderly: Differences in Depression." In *Handbook on Ethnicity, Aging, and Mental Health,* edited by Deborah K. Padgett, pp. 73-98. Westport, Conn.: Greenwood, 1995.

Turner, T. "Anthropology and Multiculturalism: What Is Anthropology That Multiculturalists Should Be Mindful of It?" In *Multiculturalism: A*

Critical Reader, edited by David T. Goldberg, pp. 406-25. Oxford: Blackwell, 1994.

Tutu, Desmond. *No Future Without Forgiveness.* New York: Doubleday, 1999.

Uchida, Yoshiko. *Desert Exile: The Uprooting of a Japanese-American Family.* Seattle: University of Washington Press, 1984.

United Church of Christ. *Resolution Regarding Reparations for Slavery.* Paper presented at the Illinois Conference of the United Church of Christ, DeKalb, Illinois, June 2002.

U.S. Department of Labor. *Breaking the Glass Ceiling.* Washington, D.C.: U.S. Government Printing Office, 1993.

Usry, Glenn, and Craig S. Keener. *Black Man's Religion: Can Christianity Be Afrocentric?* Downers Grove, Ill.: InterVarsity Press, 1996.

Vacc, Nicholas A., Susan B. Devaney and Joe Wittmer. *Experiencing and Counseling Multicultural and Diverse Populations.* Bristol, Penn.: Accelerated Development, 1995.

Vincent, L. "Watts, Rising." *World* 16 (2001): 22-25.

Virtanen, Simo, and Leonie Huddy. "Old-Fashioned Racism and New Forms of Racial Prejudice." *The Journal of Politics* 60, no. 2 (1998): 311-32.

Volf, Miroslav. *Exclusion and Embrace: A Theological Exploration of Identity, Otherness, and Reconciliation.* Nashville: Abingdon, 1996.

Voye, L. "Secularization in a Context of Advanced Modernity." *Sociology of Religion* 60, no. 3 (1999): 275-88.

Walker, Samuel, Cassia Spohn and Miriam DeLone. *The Color of Justice: Race, Ethnicity and Crime in America.* Belmont, Calif.: Wadsworth, 1999.

Wang, G.-z., and M. D. Buffalo. "Social and Cultural Determinants of Attitudes Toward Abortion: A Test of Reiss' Hypotheses." *Social Science Journal* 41, no. 1 (2004): 93-105.

Washington, Raleigh, and Glen Kehrein. *Breaking Down Walls: A Model for Reconciliation in an Age of Strife.* Chicago: Moody Press, 1993.

Watson, C. W. *Multiculturalism*. Philadelphia: Open University Press, 2000.

Weisberg, Jacob. "Thin Skins." *The New Republic*, February 18, 1991, p. 23.

West, Cornell. *Race Matters*. New York: Vintage Books, 1994.

Westley, Robert. "Many Billions Gone: Is It Time to Reconsider the Case for Black Reparations?" In *Should America Pay? Slavery and the Raging Debate on Reparations*, edited by Raymond A. Winbush. New York: Amistad, 2003.

Wheeler, Marjorie S., editor. *One Woman One Vote: Rediscovering the Woman Suffrage Movement*. Portland, Ore.: New Sage, 1995.

Whitfield, Stephen J. "America's Melting Pot Ideal and Horace Kallen." *Society* 36, no. 6 (1999): 53-55.

Wildman, Stephanie M., and Adrienne D. Davis. "Making Systems of Privilege Visible." In *White Privilege: Essential Readings on the Other Side of Racism*, edited by Paula S. Rothenberg, pp. 89-95. New York: Worth, 2002.

Wilkinson, Doris. "Minority Women: Social-Cultural Issues." In *Women and Psychotherapy*, edited by Annette M. Brodsky and Rachel T. Hare-Mustin, pp. 295-97. New York: Guilford, 1980.

Wilson, William J. *The Declining Significance of Race*. Chicago: University of Chicago Press, 1980.

Woloch, Nancy. *Women and the American Experience: A Concise History*. 2nd ed. Boston: McGraw-Hill, 2002.

Woodley, Randy. *Living in Color: Embracing God's Passion for Diversity*. Downers Grove, Ill.: InterVarsity Press, 2004.

———. *Mixed Blood Not Mixed Up: Finding God-Given Identity in a Multicultural World*. Hayden, Ala.: Eagle's Wings Ministry, 2000.

Wright, Richard. "The Ethics of Living Jim Crow: An Autobiographical Sketch." In *Race, Class and Gender in the United States,* edited by Paula S. Rothenberg. New York: Worth, 2001.

Wu, Frank. *Yellow: Race in America Beyond Black and White.* New York: Basic Books, 2003.

Yancey, George. *Beyond Black and White: Reflections on Racial Reconciliation.* Grand Rapids: Baker, 1996.

———. "Ethnocultural Allodynia or White Ignorance? How Multiracial Couples Deal with Contrasting Racial Realities." Paper presented at the National Association for Ethnic Studies, Chicago, 2005.

———. *One Body, One Spirit: Principles of Successful Multiracial Churches.* Downers Grove, Ill.: InterVarsity Press, 2003.

———. "Racial Attitudes: Differences in Racial Attitudes of People Attending Multiracial and Uniracial Congregations." *Research in the Social Scientific Study of Religion* 12 (2001): 185-206.

———. "Rubbing Off on Each Other: Close Interracial Friendships, Integrated Friendship Networks and Racial Attitudes." Unpublished paper.

———. *Who Is White? Latinos, Asians, and the New Black/Nonblack Divide.* Boulder, Colo.: Lynne Rienner Publishers, 2003.

Yancey, George, Michael O. Emerson and Karen Chai Kim. "A Comparison of How European Americans and African Americans Define Racism and Racial Prejudice." Paper presented at the Southwestern Social Science Association, Galveston, Texas, 2000.

Zhan, D., R. Eric and M. Norwich. "Churches in Action." *Leadership Journal* (Spring 2003): 41-42.